Charles Brierly Garside

Discourses on Some Parables of the New Testament

Charles Brierly Garside

Discourses on Some Parables of the New Testament

ISBN/EAN: 9783744797122

Printed in Europe, USA, Canada, Australia, Japan

Cover: Foto ©Lupo / pixelio.de

More available books at **www.hansebooks.com**

DISCOURSES

ON SOME

Parables of the New Testament.

BY

CHARLES BRIERLEY GARSIDE, M.A.

PRIEST OF THE DIOCESE OF WESTMINSTER;
FORMERLY
SCHOLAR AND HULME'S EXHIBITIONER OF BRASENOSE COLLEGE, OXFORD.

"Sapiens . . . . in absconditis Parabolarum conversabitur."
Ecclus. xxxix. 3.

LONDON:
BURNS, OATES, AND COMPANY,
17, 18 Portman Street and 63 Paternoster Row.

To

Edward Bellasis,

Serjeant-at-Law,

this Volume is affectionately dedicated

by the Author,

in grateful appreciation of a Friendship

which grows more precious with the advance of years,

and

however long may be the duration of life,

will always seem to have been

too brief.

PREFACE.

These Sermons were originally preached by the Author, during Penitential Seasons, to a miscellaneous congregation. His readers will therefore not expect from him, under these circumstances, any treatment of his subjects involving erudition and critical analysis. His aim has been simply as follows—to impress a few important truths of a practical character upon the conscience; and, at the same time, to interest the imagination in their behalf by developing, with some minuteness of detail, the imagery of the three Parables which form the contents of this volume. In preparing the work for the press, the opportunity has been taken of making some changes and additions.

CONTENTS.

The Prodigal Son.

		PAGE
I.	SIN; ITS SELFISHNESS	1
II.	SIN; A PERVERSION OF GOD'S GIFTS	20
III.	SIN; ITS WASTEFULNESS	39
IV.	SIGNS OF REPENTANCE	57
V.	HUMILITY AND SINCERITY	77
VI.	MERCY AND TRUST	98

The Sower.

I.	THE SOWER: HIS PERSON AND OFFICE	119
II.	PROFESSION WITHOUT EARNESTNESS	138
III.	EVIL THOUGHTS	159
IV.	SHALLOWNESS IN RELIGION	177
V.	THREE ENEMIES OF THE SOUL	204

The Ten Virgins.

		PAGE
I.	Dignity and Responsibility of the Christian	231
II.	Naturalism and Unreality.	251
III.	Preparation and Presumption	281

THE PRODIGAL SON.

I.

SIN; ITS SELFISHNESS.

"Father, give me the portion of substance that falleth to me." *Luke* xv. 12.

THERE are some pictures which we exhaust by one look: all that is to be seen we take in with the eye at a moment, and then pass on. There are other pictures at which we never tire of looking, because every time we examine the canvas we find out some new beauty. Such pictures as these are perpetually feeding the mind through the eye: though they are silent, yet they speak to us as though they were alive; and when our eyes have mouldered in the dust, they will continue to speak to others who follow us, teaching and delighting them in the same gentle but striking way, as they did formerly ourselves. Can we not truly say the same thing of the Parables of our Divine Lord? For what is a Gospel-parable but a picture of divine thoughts in human words?—a picture of some one important truth, or of a whole group of truths, which our Lord wishes to place before our souls in such a manner that, almost without knowing it, we are instructed, reproved, and conscience-smitten, whilst at the same time our imagination is intensely gratified.

With this short preface, let us proceed to consider the parable of the Prodigal Son. I am aware that it must be familiar to most, if not all of you; nevertheless, as I said just now of some pictures, though well known, it can be still better known; for every word and every detail is full of meaning. Even if it be familiar, what then? Is not bread familiar?—yet it is the staff of life. Are not light and air familiar?—yet without them we should wail in the darkness, and die. Are not the faces of our best and most intimate friends familiar? Nevertheless, who on that account would count such things as of little value, or love them less?

The first point to which I desire to call your attention is the utter unreasonableness of the Prodigal's conduct. Look at the position in life which the Prodigal holds. He is no wretched outcast, forced to wander because he has no home to shelter him from the scorching sun or keen wintry blast; he is no nameless being, the fruit of shame, driven about on the rough roads of the world, without a mother or a father to own him as their child; he is no slave, to whom any change is better than the whip and the chain; he is not tortured by disease, so that he hopes to escape from pain by flying to a foreign and more genial clime; nor has life become a restless burden to him, because old age has worn out the bloom and spirit of existence. Everything is exactly the opposite. He has a father full of tenderness, and who provides him with everything needful; he has even hired servants to wait upon his wants; he has a noble mansion to dwell in, and his limbs glow with all the fire of ardent youth. What means, then, this determination to leave his father's house? What secret, lying hidden beneath that eager face, draws him away like a mysterious invisible magnet, to the astonishment of the entire household? How comes that blot on the hitherto fair page of the boy's history? How is it that the father, who has often before taken delight in watching the budding growth of his son, has now to turn away and weep over the folly that he cannot, with all his persuasions, stop? For surely, though we are not told so in the parable, that father, so loving and gentle as he was, must have wept bitter tears when he looked on his child, now so full of vigour, now so radiant with excitement, and then thought of the beggary, and the hunger, and the dishonour which he prophetically saw looming in the distance. What, I ask, turned that youth into what he afterwards became? The answer to this question will cast much light upon the nature of all sin: it will tell us much, both about its motive and its character.

The spirit of evil that moved the Prodigal was manifold in its operation, but may be traced up summarily into one fountain-head—

an excessive love of self. A passion for self blinded him to everything sacred. That he had some affection for his father cannot be questioned. He calls him by the name of "father," and outwardly shows him no disrespect. Not a word of insult falls from his lips: he does not ridicule anything in the management of the household; nor does he, as some young men do, tell his father to his face that he defies him. Nevertheless, there are ways of treating others, which are cutting and disrespectful in the most intense degree, without much show of rudeness or violence. There is a cool, dogged, business-like way of claiming what we want, without taking any heed whatever of considerations which ought to make us pause. "Father, give me the portion of substance that falleth to me." There is no hesitation here, no asking whether such a proposal would be pleasing or wise. The father's feelings are not consulted for a moment: he is simply ignored and walked over. Although the son knows that his father's blood is in his veins, although he knows that but for him he would have *no goods at all*, yet one thing the Prodigal is determined upon; and what is this? Independence. "My father is noble and good," he says to himself. "He never treated me ill; and as long as I choose to stay near him, I am more than welcome. But I love something better than my father—I love myself, I love liberty. Whilst my father has any control over me and my goods, I feel not to be sufficiently my own master. The kindest, tenderest looks are ever glancing from my father's eye; but I had rather be under *no* eye. My father's rule is just and mild; but I thirst to be under *no rule at all.* 'Give me my portion of goods,' and let me go! I cannot enjoy myself unless I am more free."

This accursed love of independence is at the bottom of all sin. What is sin if it be not a rebellion against the law of God? it is the refusal to let God our heavenly Father govern our heart and mind; and what is this but an assertion that we are not under the reign of God? what is it but saying, True, God *is* my Father; but *He* must give way to *me*, and not I to Him? This language sounds monstrous when stated thus plainly; and it is language which the sinner does not use in direct terms. Neither did the Prodigal: he was in words respectful; but he looked his father full in the face without a blush whilst he asked quietly for his goods, and then he went his way. He made a reverential obeisance, no doubt; yet he turned his back upon his father without a pang.

And you, Christian sinner! Catholic sinner! is not this the very thing which you do? You, too, are in a certain sense respectful; you acknowledge in words that God is your Father. "Our Father," you say; you believe there is but one God, and therefore that He alone is your Creator and Master: "I believe in *one* God, Creator of heaven and earth." You make the sign of the Cross, and therefore every time you do so, you confess that Christ bought you with His own precious blood. You do all this; and yet, alas, when a strong desire for something forbidden by God seizes you, how do you *act?* You act as if for the moment there was no God; you determine that you will be free; and for the sake of that lawless independence, you lose that God Whom you thus pass by without regard. You are independent; that is to say, you have cut the rope that held you to the land, and you are drifting into the ocean without a rudder or a compass.

Besides this selfish love of liberty, the Prodigal was the prey of another passion. He wanted to "see the world," as it is called. His father's house was the abode of innocence and peace; everywhere reigned order, everywhere was concord, everywhere abundance. The Prodigal could not deny this; still he was not content; a fever of curiosity began by little and little to smoulder within him. "Why," he said, "should I be always living within these safe but wearisome limits? Why should I be ever doing the same round of duties, obeying the same rules? I am tired of this tasteless sameness; the very goodness of my father and his friends palls upon me. I will go out and roam like the wild-deer, finding pastures in pleasanter lands. I will have merry companions, though there be, perhaps, some echo of the Evil-one's devilry in their unchastened laughter; and I will quaff the wine-bowl of delight, though there be a risk of poison in the fumes. This body of mine, so strong and vigorous, shall have full swing; no check shall be put upon the appetites of the flesh; and this mind of mine shall soar as high and dive as deep as it likes, even into knowledge that cannot be touched without leaving a plague-spot on the soul. Nature shall have her wild gallop unrestrained. Why not?"

The history of this Prodigal is the history of many and many a soul whom the restless love of some new pleasure or new companion or new scene has led into mortal sin. Thousands are there of young men and women who owe their eternal damnation to yielding to this temptation. There is no mistaking the sign of the disease. When hearts that were before quiet begin to stir with a strange fluttering and uneasiness; when situations that were liked before begin to appear full of disagreeables;

when good steady friends are cast off and new ones, more amusing, taken up; when work and pleasure change places, the thought of enjoyment coming first, and of work afterwards, —it is a sign that a thirst for " seeing life" is coming on.

It is a bad symptom when the young want to leave their parents' home, and get rid of their watchfulness, before duty, clearly seen, calls them away; it is a bad symptom when fathers and mothers are taunted with knowing nothing, and their presence is felt to be an irksome burden; it is a bad symptom when secret acquaintanceships are made, and clandestine meetings take place away from the eye of those who would and could shield their children from danger; it is a bad symptom when that is counted insufferably dull in which there is nothing to excite the passions; and when places of amusement are sought out and eagerly entered, where they who so enter them would be sorry to be called upon suddenly to die. These are bad signs, for they show that the spirit of the Prodigal is at work. Beware, my friends, especially the young, of letting that spirit have the dominion over your hearts. You say you mean no harm; you only want to have a little variety, you want a frolic now and then for your mind and body; you cannot, you say, be always considering what sort of persons you are going to meet. You know well that whilst reading certain books and tales, you would start with fear if you saw your Guardian-Angel suddenly looking over your shoulder, as with a feverish pleasure you suck in the poison cunningly mixed with the honey. But you say, " Who can be always keeping their curiosity under lock and key?" Then, again, with regard to these places of amusement, where so much evil is plotted, and where characters mingle freely in the company whose names smell rank with dishonour: "O," you say, "*we* have no concern with *them;* we go not for sin, but for amusement; we just take a hasty run from our dull homes, to have a peep at life, and then are back again without fail." My dear friends, what you *mean* God alone and your conscience can thoroughly know; but what *happens* is too often this. In seeing what you call life, you are blinded by the vapour of a spiritual death; you frolic until you roll over the edge of the gulf into mortal sin; you harness the thoughtless passionate spirits of youth to the car of Pleasure, and say, Drive on; away; fast! Yes, you and your companions drive on —on into the darkness, quicker and quicker, the darkness growing deeper and deeper. But mark! unseen, unheeded by you, who are too busy to be on your guard, there mounts at your side one whose look if you beheld it, would strike you dead with terror. He is close to you; closer than man can be to his brother man; he takes your hands into his; and whilst you fondly dream that *you* are still driving, it is *he* who guides the reins. It is that nameless horror, the Evil One—Satan himself. You need no sign-post to tell you whither he is taking you. Ask the tigress whither she is dragging her prey. Is it not to her lair, where the ground is rough with the whitened bones of her victims? Satan is driving you fast to his own dreadful home, the sound of the wheels being muffled, amid the jingling music of your evil merriment.

The next point to be remarked in the conduct of the Prodigal is the exceedingly unworthy way in which he estimated his father's value. The link that binds a child to a parent is something so wonderful, so close, and so mysterious that it reminds one of that which exists between the Creator and the creature. But for that father the youth would have had no place in the world of things; he would have had no soul to think with, no body to move about with upon the earth; the goods he asked for, and the power to use them, were in truth owing to that father. One would have thought that the very sound of his own voice, when he said "Father," would have struck a chord in his heart, and made him acknowledge the dignity and the sacredness of his parent's office. The son, alas, treated the father as the selfish treat all men and all things. He looked at his father simply as a means to an end; that end was his own will—the gratification of his corrupt self. Just as a man looks on a bank-note, and says to himself, "It is only paper, but it is good for so much gold;" in some similar manner did this young man regard his father. If his father had not been able to give him the means of enjoying himself, he would have cared little about him. We can well imagine him, when the goods came to be distributed, watching each portion as it was delivered out, weighing and counting every item; and then when the goods were safely in his possession, heaving a sigh that the father's office was over as agent and provider of his son's ungenerous wants. So did the love of self blind and harden the heart of one who had as yet not even seen that dangerous outer world which he so eagerly wished to enter.

You will all agree with me that the conduct of the Prodigal was unnatural and mean. I know that an honest feeling of just indignation is rising within you as, in fancy, you compare the selfish coolness of the one with the noble generosity of the other, who robbed himself prematurely of what he might have kept, in order that the son should never be able to charge the father with a want of regard for his child. If you came across such a son, you feel that you could not resist rebuking him in strong language for his unkindness and his greediness. Now, look steadily into this part of the parable; perhaps, if you fix your gaze well, you will see that the page changes into a mirror; and in this mirror you will behold, not the Prodigal of the past and his earthly father, but *yourself.* Yes; look well,—is it not yourself? Instead of the human parent, the parent made of dust, who is it that stands there before the eye of conscience? Is it not *God*—God your Creator, God the almighty One, God the merciful One, God the Father of all?

You are His children, are you not? Tell me, then, whether you have not too often treated Him as the Prodigal treated *his* father? Have you never, by your conduct, acted in a selfish way towards God? Have you not often enjoyed the goods He has given you without once thinking whence they came, and to whom you were answerable for their right use? Is not God, alas, perpetually treated as only a *means* to an end, and not as the First Beginning and Last End? The Prodigal did not deny that the good things he received came through the hands of his parent; nor do you deny that *all* you have that is good—soul and body, food, raiment, time for repentance, and, above all, grace and redemption—you do not deny that these things come from God. You would be infidels, if you did; but as the Prodigal looked at his father as only a *channel* to pass on to himself this stream of gifts, and when he had received them, cared no more for the giver, so is it not a sad truth that *you*, whilst possessing all kinds of blessings both of body and soul, have forgotten *God Himself*, from whom they came?

Hence it is that the Lord, through the lips of His prophet Moses, uttered this bitter complaint against the people of Israel, for whom He had done so much: "Hear, O ye heavens, the things I speak; let the earth give ear to the words of My mouth. Is this the return thou makest to the Lord, O foolish and senseless people? is not He thy Father that hath possessed thee, and made thee, and created thee?

Thou hast forsaken the Lord that begat thee; thou hast forgotten the Lord that created thee" (Deut. xxxii.).

If you have never wilfully sinned, then I admit that you stand acquitted of the charge which I make. But who will dare to say that he has never wilfully sinned? "If we say," writes St. John, "that we have no sin, we deceive ourselves, and the truth is not in us." You have sinned, then, and as sinners I address you. Now, all sin whatever that is committed, is committed by our using some good thing in a way contrary to the will of God. The intemperate man sins by using to a wicked excess that food or drink that in itself is good, but which is turned into iniquity by his own abuse; the liar uses his power of speech contrary to the will of God, which declares that the lips must speak truth; the thief misuses property, which in itself is a gift of God to those who rightfully possess it; the impure man uses the passions and forces of his body in a way forbidden by Him Who created the wonderful building of the body in order that it should be the temple of the Holy Ghost: in each case you will find that sin is a wicked appropriation to our own selfish purpose of something which God has given us to be used solely for His glory. Whoever therefore sins does by that very act treat God, not as the Sovereign Ruler and Disposer of the goods which come from Him, but simply as a channel through which they are obtained. Hence the weighty conclusion, that by sin the very order of nature is reversed; for instead of treating God as the all-supreme, all-glorious Creator and Father, the sinner, without saying so in words, really *acts* as if God only existed in order to supply the means for enabling the sinner to commit evil; as though the Creator only lived in order to enable the creature to break the laws of creation, and cloud that glory which he was destined to manifest and advance throughout the world.

"Father," said the Prodigal, "give me the portion of goods that falleth to me." And when he had obtained the goods, he seemed to think that he had no more concern with the intention of his father in giving them than if he had received them from a senseless piece of matter—from a field or a tree, or a mine of stone or metal. Forget not, therefore, that the goods you possess have the Master's stamp indelibly fixed upon them, and can never be used against the Master's will without sin. Take heed by the example of this parable, and when you count up, if such a thing be possible, the gifts you have received from your Father in Heaven, say, "Do I always recognise my Father's mark upon them? Do I use them as a faithful son, consulting my Father's glory and honour; or do the angels see written on my forehead, in deep burning letters, Thoughtless, thankless, selfish Prodigal?"

II.

SIN; A PERVERSION OF GOD'S GIFTS.

"A few days after, the younger son, gathering all together, went abroad into a far country." *Luke* xv. 13.

FOR a few days, it appears, the future Prodigal lingered at home. It may be that sometimes a little suspicion crossed his mind that he was about to make a step more venturesome than wise. Buoyant as his youthful spirits were, intoxicated as was his imagination at the thought of the new scenes he was going to visit, and the new life he was about to begin, proud as he felt of his own boldness, which by a fond delusion he mistook for true manliness, still, no doubt, a shadow would occasionally creep over the brightness of his dream. When he met his father's eye, he could not conceal from himself that he beheld in that look a tender sadness, which was painfully prophetic. Just as men, who are uneasy through some haunting fear, try to laugh it away, but in spite of all, cannot quite succeed, so this youth experienced a certain misgiving which would not always keep away. There were moments in the still hush of the night when this question came, like an unbidden spirit, before his soul: Am I right to forsake my father, and to banish myself from my home for the sake of pleasure and liberty?—this question would come, till at last he coaxed or drove it away, and took his rest in sleep and forgetfulness. Then in the sunny morning, when everything was cheerful, and people were moving about, and there were many things to be arranged, this disquieting question would be thought of no more; he was too busy to hear its voice. So in the end, after a little hesitation, and balancing, and lingering, just to show that his will was free, the love of self weighed down the scale. The world carried the day triumphantly; the treasures which his father had given him prevailed against the father himself, and robbed him of his son. The youth decided to leave his father rather than part with his father's gifts; so he "gathered them all together," and went away "into a far country."

He "gathered *all* together" with a miserly exactness: not one particle of property did he leave behind; not the smallest trifle as a pledge of his return; not one single thing for his father to use if he was so disposed. All were gathered together, because all were intended to carry out one purpose—they were to be so many servants to supply his gratifications. He drew them all to himself, as their centre and their end.

As far as we can determine from the parable, there does not appear to have been a deliberate intention from the very first to spend this property in vice; although the parable states that he did so in the end, when he had arrived in "the far country;" for there, we are told, he wasted his substance, living riotously.

Now, in this part of the Prodigal's history, we can read a very important lesson. The father, as I have before explained, represents Almighty God; and the portion of substance or property that fell to the son's share, represents everything which God has given to man upon earth. Of these things not one is evil in itself, otherwise we should make God the author of evil. But such is the nature of these goods, that if they are not used as God intended them to be used, they will inevitably draw man into sin. In order to understand how this happens, you must bear in mind that nothing whatever in the world is made for itself, just as nothing whatever can subsist by itself. We are exceedingly apt to forget that the tiniest as well as the mightiest creatures would all sink into nothingness if God were to withdraw His support. In the language of Scripture, God upholds all things by His power: yet who thinks of this as he ought? Who remembers that if for one millionth part of a moment God were to withdraw His all-sustaining hand, the entire universe would be gone—gone quicker than the quickest flash of lightning? Our eyes do not see the hand of God, nor do our ears catch the sound of His quickening presence throughout creation,—nevertheless *God is there.* Equally true is it, that as all things are made by Him, and are upheld by Him, they are made and upheld but for one purpose—to serve and glorify Him. Nothing can be neutral; because nothing can withdraw itself from the dominion of God. Does anything exist? then it must be for God; and if it be not employed for Him, then it is used against Him.

Supposing, therefore, that we have no fixed intention to use our time, our money, our talents, our influence, our opportunity, and the like, in the perpetration of vice, this is not enough to free us from guilt. That we are bound not to pervert these gifts to vice is certain, but we are also bound to see that the gifts we possess, whether of mind, body, or of the world, are employed for their proper end. *We*, I say, are so bound, because we are what we are—*men*. Man has a great, but for that very reason a deeply responsible, position in the world. He does not stand in the world as an idle or curious looker-on only; nor does he stand, as if he were only an item in a large quantity of things; like a stone in a quarry, or a tree among other trees of the forest. Man is a member of the world of nature; but he is far

Sin; a Perversion of God's Gifts. 25

more. He is the guardian, the great spokesman of nature; for all things created have two ways of glorifying God. They glorify Him by being what they are, as works of God. Thus, even the flowers of the field, and the stars in the firmament, and animals without reasonable souls, glorify God; and this kind of service no one can take from them. They serve God by existing: "Here we are," they say; "and by being here at all, we proclaim the presence and power and wisdom of the Creator." This service will last as long as they last; it is a service that would go on just the same if not a man breathed on the face of the globe; it is the cry of nature to God, saying, "Father," although none but God hears the sound.

The second and higher way of glorifying God is when the works of nature—all created things, in short—serve and glorify God by serving man, who being made in the image of God, is bound to employ them in such a way that they shall carry out God's plan in creation. The instant they come under man's touch, man must direct them to the glory of God, which is at the same time his own true glory, and a means to him of sanctification. Man is therefore charged with an office of amazing dignity; for he is to be, as it were, the living altar on which other created things of the world are to be laid and offered up as a sweet-smelling incense to God.

It is not enough, therefore, for anyone to say, in respect to the gifts he possesses through the providence of God, "I will not pollute you by offering you up to Satan;" nor is it enough to say, "I will leave you alone, and do nothing with you." This is not enough, because we are all bound by the strictest law to offer them to God. The creatures of God may be compared to some wondrously exquisite harp. If no gifted fingers are ready to reveal its powers by their magic touch, then let the zephyrs break the silence, and weave a sweet though inferior melody of their own, as they wander over the chords.

If, however, a musician with a soul and intelligence be present, and who is able to play on that harp divinely, surely it should be his honourable ambition and delight to draw from its mechanism harmonies worthy of the instrument and its artificer. So nature, without man, will sing its own hymn of praise to God; but when man comes in, then from his power and skill God expects a canticle of adoration worthy of nature, worthy of man, and worthy of God.

Although, then, you may not have quite made up your minds to turn the created things which you possess, such as your time, your thoughts, your understanding, your affections, your money, your opportunities, and the like, into downright sin, still you are guilty before God for that very hesitation. Because to leave it even *undetermined* whether you will employ the things of this world to their one and only end, namely, the will of God, is itself a deadly mistake. Nor is this all; for beside this indifference being wrong, it is sure to lead to still further sin. Live in this world, only for a few hours, without any kind of idea that you are bound to use what you find here to the glory of God, and you cannot help sinning. You are not angels, unable to be influenced by this world; you are not saints in heaven, to whom everything is poor except the Face of God, which they behold. You are men; frail, corruptible, and tempted every minute; overborne perhaps by long-practised evil habits that have become a second nature to you. What will happen, then, if you forget the very end of the creation in the midst of which you live? This will happen: the things you see before you, which you touch, and hear; things perfectly innocent in themselves, such as food, clothing, friends, knowledge, beauty of all kinds, health and strength,—all these things will be a snare to you. If you do not by a pure intention turn them to the honour of God, they will drag you down to their own level. You are in a stream, and if you do not look to the compass, and keep the ship perpetually steering towards the one port, then the very wind which would have taken you home in full sail, and the very waters on which you would have been borne safely along, will be your enemies. That which happens sometimes to the mariner will happen to you. Are you imagining that although you are not using the world for God, yet you are not using it *against* Him? This is a delusive fiction.

So the sailor sometimes flatters himself, that if he be not going direct to port, yet he is not going away from it; he is moving pleasantly about, when all of a sudden he is startled from his sleep by a crash upon the rocks. Never fancy that there is no danger because you are not conscious of using this world directly *against* God; are you using it *for* Him? if not, then you may be sure that you, too, are drifting among the rocks.

As long as the Prodigal in the Gospel was with his father, we do not hear of his wasting his substance. He was ready to do so, because he was ready to leave his father. But the grosser iniquity did not begin until he was away from home, and saw nothing before his eyes except his goods. In this little fact, I think we can trace a confirmation of what I have been saying. If we have the thought of God our Father present to our soul, we shall not so easily forget that the world in which we live is made for His glory. Remember God, and you will remember that for Him your own self, and all things with which you have to do, were made. But let the thought of God become rare, and then dim will grow your remembrance of the true use of the world. You will see in it what the Prodigal saw in the good things he carried away—nothing but a means of furnishing you with power and pleasure; a view of the world utterly false, deceitful, and dishonouring to God.

After leaving his father the next thing we are told about the Prodigal is, that he went abroad "into a far country." Why into a far country? Was it his intention from the outset, as he stood for the last time on the threshold, whilst he turned his face towards the open plain before him? Did he say to himself, "I will not be content with going a short distance; I will go, if need be, over high mountains; I will cross swollen rivers; I will brave the fiery heats of the desert; I will go as far as I can, where no messenger from my father can find me, and no inquiries can reach me from friends"? Most probably he had no such idea. He wanted to enjoy himself, and to have plenty of liberty, but had no fixed plan besides. But somehow or other he went a long way, and found himself in another land altogether. I daresay he kept his youthful spirits up well with anticipations of what was in store for him; and as he passed along and saw new things, new persons, and new customs, he wandered on without at all measuring his distance. The present, the bright, sunny, merry present, was everything to him; and he altogether forgot that a time would come when to go back would be a long and wearisome journey.

Behold a picture of the man who is bent on pleasing himself. Like the Prodigal, he cannot do this without leaving God. When I say that he leaves God, I of course do not mean that he leaves the presence of God: he cannot leave that, however he may try; the power of God is ever in him, and acting through him: "Whither shall I go from Thy Spirit? or whither shall I flee from Thy face? If I ascend into heaven, Thou art there; if I descend into hell, Thou art there" (Ps. cxxxviii. 8). The lost in hell cannot escape from the presence of God. When a man follows his own desires, without any regard to God's will, he leaves God by his affections; he forgets Him in his heart: as St. Augustin says, "To desert God is to forget Him." At first there seems no particular change in that man; his spirits are much as usual, perhaps higher than before, because of the excitement of the pleasure which he is following; nor has he any idea of going deep into the tangled forest which he has been beguiled into entering. He has no deliberate intention to stop; but he has also no deliberate intention not to stop. But one pleasure suggests another; one desertion of God's will paves the way for a fresh desertion. Onward he goes; onward and onward. To get out of one sin he commits another; the flesh pulls harder and harder, and the Spirit of God seems to draw with a force that grows weaker. At length his conscience grows dim and mystified, so that he loses his sense of distance from God. Landmarks that ought to startle him with their signs pass unmeaningly before his dreamy eye.

He knows he is outside his Father's house, but he thinks he is only a little astray; when, behold, he is "abroad in a far country"!

We may liken the Prodigal going away from his home, but not having yet passed the boundaries of his father's territory, to those who are giving way to a continued course of venial sin. They are becoming more and more distant from God, but they are as yet within the enclosure of His friendship; the link of grace and charity which binds them and Him is being stretched hard, until at last the deed of darkness is done; mortal sin is committed, the bond of friendship between the soul and its God is severed through, and in a single instant that miserable soul drops into an abyss so profound that no mortal line can fathom its depth. If there be any man, woman, or child here who is at this moment out of the state of grace; if there be any here who by neglect of Sacraments, or by breaking some law of the Church by which they are bound, or by any deed of malice, envy, or hatred, or filthiness of impurity, are in deadly sin; if there be any here of this class, to them I speak, when I declare that they are indeed, like the Prodigal, abroad in a far, far country. You lift up your eyes and think that the blue vault above is far from the bottom of the sea in its deepest part; but this is nearness compared with the distance of your soul from God, if you are in deadly sin. You are worlds and worlds apart from Him; not apart from Him as a Creator, but as a Saviour, a Friend, and a Father.

Away from God! O my friends, how dreadful must this be if you only think upon it as you ought! There are those who have died of a broken heart simply because they were obliged to stay in a foreign land; and yet the land, perhaps, was far pleasanter than their own; it was more cheerful and fertile, with greener hills and nobler rivers and wealthier inhabitants. But they pined because it was not their own native country. Yet what is any banishment from a native country, which all must leave at death, compared with exile from God? You are near parents and friends, perhaps, whom you love deeply; you are near many things that are delightful; nay, I will suppose, what is impossible, you are near the full satisfaction of your utmost ambition. Nevertheless, these things cannot change the effect of sin; they may hide the awful fact from you, but the fact remains. Your soul is in a country far from God. The Prodigal knew that he was in another land; but it is just possible that you may be away from God, and not be aware of it, because, through carelessness or self-deceit, you may think that you are in God's friendship when you are not. If you cannot deny that you are in mortal sin, then it is certain—absolutely certain —that your soul is cut off entirely from God; it is as certain as if a hand were to come forth and write your name in letters of light on the walls of your room, as the name of a son who is an outcast from heaven.

No one, who is not either insane or utterly hardened and blinded by long habits of iniquity, would really be indifferent about forsaking God. No one is so horribly blasphemous as to say, "I am *determined* to abandon God, my best Friend." Yet thousands who never say so, actually *do* so; hell is crammed with poor souls, who never in their lives deliberately said, " I will, out of sheer malice and boldness, commit a mortal sin." How comes it to pass, then, that so many die, cut off from God? Because they have not been careful to watch the movements of their passions—because they have looked on this world as a place out of which they were resolved to draw all the pleasure they possibly could, instead of looking at it as a place where all of us must "work out our salvation with fear and trembling"—because they allowed their heart to ramble wherever it chose, never checking its love for forbidden joys—because they preferred a false godless liberty to the holy yoke of Christ—because, perhaps more than all, they neither feared nor did anything to guard against venial sin. Though the way winds about a great deal, and is often disguised by our self-deceit, be assured of this: the road that leads to wilful venial sin is the same that leads to mortal; and the road of mortal sin opens direct by a very broad path to that farthest country of all—the land of the lost, from which, when once entered, there is no return. Stop, then, while you have time; stop, before you have gone to the farthest point. Give no heed to all those invitations which meet the soul at every step. "Take this one enjoyment," says the flesh, "only this *one;*" and then to-morrow we find the same flesh again coaxing us to a fresh indulgence. "You have gone thus far," says Satan, "on the road of liberty, and do you not find it pleasant? You see no harm has happened to you; come a little farther, and you will find still more enjoyment!"

You have told a falsehood, at which you blush—"Tell another," says Convenience, "and you will escape detection." You want to do an unlawful deed, but are timid; then you hear the persuasions of evil companions, saying, "How cowardly you are; how scrupulous!" And you do something far worse than you intended.

Such are the temptations that every soul meets with, and the only way to stand firm is to do what the Prodigal did not do: it is to cleave to our Father always, and to fear nothing so much as any act, word, person, place, or thought which has a tendency to separate us from Him, even if it be ever so little.

> " O good Jesu, give ear to my prayer:
> Within Thy wounds hide me,
> Nor suffer me ever to be separated from Thee."

III.

SIN; ITS WASTEFULNESS.

"He went abroad into a far country, and there wasted his substance, living riotously. And after he had spent all, there came a mighty famine in that country, and he began to be in want. And he went and cleaved to one of the citizens of that country, and he sent him into his farm to feed swine." *Luke* xv. 13-15.

AFTER arriving at the "far country," the career of the Prodigal was a rapid descent into evil. Eagerly had he received, and most carefully had he gathered to himself, the portion of substance which he had begged from his father. Often on the journey must he have thought on the variety and preciousness of these gifts. As he drove the herds of fine cattle before him, and unrolled the splendid garments which had fallen to his share, and whose rich softness and embroidery had been the pride of his father's household; and as he counted, often for security and also for pleasure, his gold and silver pieces, and the jewels which trustworthy attendants carried for him secured in caskets, often must the reflection have crossed his mind, that he was bearing away things of great value, things that had been for many long years collected one by one, at no small cost of labour and anxiety on the part of his father. Alas, little did that father ever expect beforehand how ungratefully one son at least would treat him; little did he imagine that what had been gained by so much labour, and preserved with so much care, would be scattered with so much recklessness! Yet so it was; for the Prodigal, we are told, "wasted his substance, living riotously." Although every article he spent must have reminded him of his father; although he knew well how that father's heart would bleed if he could only see what his son was doing, nevertheless he went on consuming his goods. Each day he saw his substance was becoming less and less; it was vanishing like smoke; still no reproachful memories of his forsaken home, no consideration even of honour, no suggestions of prudence, stopped him. Like a man blindfold and mad, he never rested until he had "spent *all*," to the last farthing.

Have *you* ever considered the preciousness and the sacredness of that substance which *you* waste when you give way to sin? When we see things of this earth turned from their proper use, and employed in ways utterly unworthy of their destined purpose, we all feel indignation, nay, more than indignation; for in the great perversion of some valuable object we feel, by an instinct, as if something out of the order of nature, some monstrosity had been committed. What would you think if, when thousands were starving, whole granaries of corn were to be given to the flames in order to make a festive blaze? What would you think if garments sumptuous enough for a Solomon were to be strewed broadcast, for wild cattle to trample upon and defile?

What would you think if a splendid temple were to be given up to be the abode of the most loathsome reptiles, or the most foul and unsightly of birds? In these and kindred instances, everyone would shrink from the base unnaturalness of the action. Yet no perversion, no waste of any mere earthly substance, can be compared to that produced by sin. Do you ask *what* it is that sin wastes? Rather ask what it is that it does *not* waste. Sin is not like a sound that passes off and leaves no trace behind. Sin is the act of a sinner; and a sinner is a living man, who has much to do with the world. He is a man who breathes the air, who enjoys the sun's light, who is supported by the food which the earth supplies; he is a man for whom the vast machinery of creation is always working in one way or another. Sin, then, is a waste of the world in which the sinner lives; if all the things which a sinner uses merely as a man, merely to enable him to continue life, were to have a voice given them, they would cry out in an agony of indignation, " You are ruling us tyrannically; you are robbing us; you are destroying us, for we were made originally for man, and not for sinners." Again, sin is an iniquitous waste of time; we cannot live without time; our very consciousness of life is measured by our notion of hours and minutes. Now the moment we reflect, we perceive the

Sin; its Wastefulness.

amazing value of this gift. Upon time all things here and hereafter depend. There is a well-known saying, that time is money; it is far more, for in one sense it is everything. What is the use of air if you have no time to breathe? of gold, if you have no time to exchange it for something else? What is the use of prayer, of repentance, of grace itself, without time? The very Blood of Christ, which opens the gates of heaven, can do nothing for me if my last minute is gone before that Blood can be applied. If such is time, it is hard to imagine anything more valuable. Woe to anyone that dishonours it! woe to anyone that despises it! woe to anything that robs it from us! woe to anything that perverts it! Then woe to sin! For what is the chief waster of time, but sin? The chief, did I say? This is far below the truth; for sin, and sin alone, is able to waste time. How could it be otherwise? Were you not born to adore and serve God? When the hand of the Almighty brought you out of nothing; when He said, "Be MAN; not some tiny insect which hardly lives till the sun sets that beamed upon its birth, but MAN; be MAN; be immortal; be intended for the companionship of My angels—nay more, be intended to become eternal kings and priests in heaven; partakers of the divine nature and of My joy;" when God thus acted out of His boundless mercy and wisdom, did He not mean that the years, weeks, days, and hours which He allotted to you should be employed in His service?

If, then, you employ even the sixtieth part of a minute in a sinful imagination, you are spending in a way contrary to the will of God that which is given to you for the sole purpose of enabling you to do that will. What a thought, moreover, it is for us all—a thought full of humiliation—that we, rational beings, we who are so vainly proud of our superiority to the lower creatures, are the only ones who *do* and who *can* waste the time that God has given us! Look at those reptiles which remain inactive for months, with scarcely a movement, and whose whole life seems spent in gorging their prey and then slumbering till they gorge it again; and those other creatures too, more active and restless, who seem to exist only to destroy their kindred species; none of these *waste* the treasure of time because, however they act, having no free will and no conscience, they cannot use their days and hours *against* the will of their Creator. It is the sinner alone who is guilty of this unnatural act.

There is another unholy waste which we are too apt to forget—the loss of all the merits which we may have hitherto gained through the mercy and grace of God. The merits that a soul acquires whilst in a state of grace are immense. He who counts the very hairs of our head, He who forgets not "the cup of cold water given to a disciple in His name," He alone can tell what jewels a soul is adding to its future crown by every earnest prayer, by every act of self-control, by every movement towards God. And as God alone can tell what the actual degree of merit is in any particular soul up to the time of mortal sin, so He alone can measure the graces that He was keeping ready for it, as a further reward for the merit already gained. "To him that hath shall be given." Such is the promise of God. We may say of each fresh merit that it draws after itself a continually increasing chain of new graces, which God delights in allowing (if we may use such an expression) to lie loose in His hands, and ready to be let down to us from heaven. Imagine, too—no, I must ask you to try to imagine,—for to understand it worthily is impossible,—try to imagine, then, the joy of Jesus, the joy of Mary, the joy of all the saints and angels, whenever a soul makes even one act of Christian virtue; because each act adorns that soul with a greater beauty, and enables God to draw it closer into His own embrace. Consider all this; consider the merits already gained, the new graces that are on their way, bringing to the soul fresh light, purity and love, and the joys of the whole court of heaven steadily increasing. Conceive all this, and then remember that one single mortal sin saps everything to the foundation, ruins all, sweeps all away. What a destruction! All the treasures in all the richest merchant ships of the world, if sunk in the sea—all the most splendid palaces, if engulfed by earthquakes, would be as the loss of a box of toys to a child, when compared with the loss which a soul suffers from one mortal sin. For who can liken the value of the love and grace of God to any mere earthly treasure, which must perish some day when the world shall be burnt up? We should think it a great sacrifice if we saw a man fling into the fire the title-deeds of a large estate, for we should imagine that we saw the houses and lands going into the flames. But mortal sin, yes, a sin of thought, which requires not a minute for its completion, does more—it tears up the title-deeds to heaven, sealed by the Blood of the Lamb Himself, and casts them contemptuously away.

The Prodigal in the Gospel knew the exact amount of what he was so wickedly consuming; but it is one of the terrible laws of sin, that no man can say how much he has lost by even one sin, still less how much he has lost by a course of evil. I have spoken of the graces and the merits he has himself forfeited; but who can tell how much damage he has inflicted upon his fellow-men? We do not live alone, and apart from others; the race of man is like a vast coil of metal, of which each circle touches and influences another, so that if you send an electric current in at one spot, it will go through the whole mass. So, when one man sins, it is impossible for the effects of that one sin to be entirely shut up in himself. Who is to put his soul into quarantine? who can stop the moral effluvium of sin? A whole train of miserable events quite unforeseen by him will most probably follow. Who can tell what mischief his own example will do? who can tell what grace has been utterly lost to numbers through the neglect of a single duty? who can tell how many will perhaps be hereafter in hell in a great measure through the fault of others? How often has an immoral parent ruined the innocence of the children, and made them in their turn bad parents, who will ruin their children too? How often does one man drag another, with the lasso of friendship, into evil, who would have been safe but for that unhappy bond of acquaintanceship? All sin is a pestilence, which the sinner carries with him wherever he goes, and scatters abroad through numerous channels without even being aware of it; just as a man in a contagious fever passes on disease to those who are within the range of his breath, whilst he himself is in a state of stupor, and is unconscious that each act of breathing, which is a sign that he still lives, is conveying the very spirit of corruption into those who stand near.

Such is sin: a terrible destroyer, not only of a man's own self, of his own body, of his own soul, of his own graces and merits, but also of the souls and bodies, of the graces and merits and the future salvation of others.

Sin is not committed for nothing. Whoever breaks the law of God does it under an impression—true or false—that he will gain some satisfaction that he would have lost if he had not committed the sin. The Prodigal exchanged his goods for riotous living, for gluttony, intemperance, and impurity. You possibly sacrifice your time, your talents, and graces for other objects; it may be for vanity,

E

or it may be for money, or it may be for revenge, or for an idle life. Whatever the object may be, there is one motive common to all sinners: they have a craving which they want to satisfy, and they expect to find that satisfaction in sin. This expectation has been in the world since the first sin in the garden of Eden; it will remain until the last sin is committed upon the earth, possibly up to within a second of the world's destruction; and it will be as false then as it is now, and as it was when Adam and Eve were deceived and ruined. Now sin may give a certain pleasure, short though it must always be; but no sin can give real satisfaction to the soul. The pleasure of sin is only like true satisfaction, as the scenes in a drama are like realities: the spectators have before them various views—trees, rocks, sea and sky, sun, moon, and stars; they behold fountains playing, kings on their thrones, armies fighting, caskets of gems, and luxurious banquets; they see everything arranged to give the impression of reality, but all is imitation: the sun is only a paper transparency, the monarch's crown a bit of tinsel, the flowing water only revolving glass; and so with the rest. Thus it is with sin, which promises to fill the soul, and only mocks it. "Why," says the Prophet, "do you spend money for that which is *not* bread, and give labour for that which doth *not* satisfy you? Hearken diligently, and eat *that which is food*, and your soul shall be delighted in fatness" (Is. lv. 2). Remember how the Prodigal fared. When his substance was most wanted, nothing remained. After he had spent all, "there came a mighty famine in that country, and he began to be in want." His wealthy and prudent father's granaries were doubtless filled to overflowing; there was no lack of oil and wine and cattle *there*. But the Prodigal was in a *far country*—away from his father. There was a *mighty famine*. We can form but a slight notion of what is summed up in that word. What matters it how fair a land is to the eye, if there be no food? What matters it how clever are its statesmen, how valiant its soldiers, how opulent its merchants, *if there be no food?* To be without food is to be without the material for life: it is to have no power in the once strong limbs; it is to have a heart whose beat becomes weaker and weaker at each stroke, and blood which moves slower and slower, and hands that lose their grasp, and eyes that glare wild in their haggard sockets, and a tongue that cleaves to the parched mouth, unable to tell articulately the misery that is going on; it is to have a reeling brain; to be tempted to acts of desperation; and to be sometimes so hardened and maddened, that mothers have been known to stagger, knife in hand to the cradle, in order to slay and devour with a horrible eagerness the very flesh of those little ones whom they have before suckled at their own breast.

In the Prodigal's land there "came a mighty famine;" and so there is always a famine whenever an unfortunate soul abandons its God. For out of God there is nothing good, nothing substantial, nothing worthy of the soul's real dignity and deep craving. The soul's hunger begins to be felt soon after it has gone astray; and the farther it wanders, the greater is the barrenness of the country. In the midst of the freshness and excitement of the beginning of sin, the reality of want may be concealed; but it is there, only waiting for time to allow it to bite more keenly. You may try and stifle the inward cry of want by distractions, and false arguments, and gaiety; just as the Hindoo victims used to be dressed out in rich robes, and crowned with flowers, in the midst of music, before they mounted their funeral-bed of fire. Still, all you can do will fail to destroy the uneasy restlessness which sin works in the heart. The Prodigal is represented as going into a land where the famine was; but, in truth, the sinner carries the famine within him wherever he goes. His own soul is the "far country" itself: it is there that the blight of selfishness is ever cankering what is good; it is there that the locusts of the passions are ever devouring and defiling the fairest of God's gifts.

O sinner, whoever you are, be you wealthier and wiser in earthly wisdom than Solomon, be you stronger in body than Samson, be your social condition a "land flowing with milk and honey," nevertheless, as long as you are in sin, you are in a state of "mighty famine." How can it be otherwise? for you are in want of all that the soul ought to possess. You want the grace of God, for you have driven it out; you want the light of God's direction, for you have chosen darkness; you want order, for you have let in chaos; you want peace, for it is impossible for peace to dwell in a heart which is at enmity with God and its own self.

There is one step more in the misery of sin besides the famine, and then the resemblance to the Prodigal is complete. To appease his growing hunger, he hired himself out to a citizen of that famine-stricken land. He, the noble father's son—he who left his father to be more free was too thankful to hire himself out; and for what purpose?—for the degrading office of tending swine, animals viewed by the Jews, to whom the parable was first addressed, with abhorrence, as unclean. Poor Prodigal! this is indeed a change from thy sumptuous table and the merry companions of thy luxurious festivities. The sparkling wines are finished, and the wanton dancings are over. All seemed to go prosperously at first, till thy substance was spent, and the dearth came. Where art thou now? Bending in tattered rags, and with gaunt cheeks, over thy filthy charge, and only wishing that the putrid garbage which the swine are crunching with pleasure *could* be thy food; which it cannot, for the refuse-husks of the sty only mock, without being able to allay, the Prodigal's hunger.

The swine feed well on their garbage because they *are* swine; and they sleep well in their mire because they have no idea of cleanliness, and no evil conscience to disturb their slumbers. But the Prodigal, although he has lived like them, has been unable entirely to forget that he is a man with a soul, with a conscience and a God. Hence his misery, and hence the misery of all those who, under the delusion of having more enjoyment and more liberty through sin, find out, alas, to their dreadful cost, that their pleasure is wormwood, their abundance a "mighty famine," and their freedom a degrading slavery. "Man, when he was in honour, did not understand: he hath been compared to senseless beasts, and hath become like unto them" (Ps. xlviii. 13). "As he that is hungry dreameth and eateth, but when he is awake his soul is empty; and as he that is thirsty dreameth and drinketh, and after he is awake is yet faint with thirst, and his soul is empty: so shall be the multitude of the gentiles that have fought against Mount Sion" (Is. xxix. 8).

IV.

SIGNS OF REPENTANCE.

"Returning to himself, he said, How many hired servants in my father's house abound in bread, and I here perish with hunger?" *Luke* xv. 17.

THE history of the Prodigal has up to the present been the history of a man labouring under a sad and powerful delusion. His common sense, his education, and his father's tenderness were unable to shield him from the infatuated career on which he had chosen to enter, in spite of every remonstrance. He started from home under an impression that away from his father he would be more happy and free. This was the first part of his dream. Not content with what he found in the "far country" to which he had wandered, with the true spirit of a gambler he kept spending more and more of his substance, in the hope of at length discovering that complete satisfaction which had hitherto never arrived,—this was the second part of the dream,—until at length all was spent, and the mighty famine came, and he began to be in want. So far the course of the Prodigal has been one continued dark page—it has seemed as if the clouds would never break; and now that the famine has spread through the whole country, and is probing him to the very quick, his sky looks blacker than ever. But have you not often noticed, at the time when the heavens are like a large funeral pall, covering all the hills and valleys, the streams, the fields, the trees and the flowers, suddenly a little corner of the pall is lifted up, and the blue vault comes forth like a new creation? So it is here: the misery of the Prodigal is the crisis of the disease. The hunger, and the slavery, and the degradation of feeding the stranger's unclean swine, at length agonise him, until he becomes alive to his real state. There are men who sometimes from disease have fallen into a sleep so profound that nothing would arouse them but the sharp piercing of a knife, or the strong shock of a galvanic battery. And had it not been for the failure of all his substance and the pangs of hunger, the Prodigal would have remained in his miserable infatuation. He would have died in the midst of his pleasure—died impenitent; he would have been buried in his sin; and though the world, which never sees below the surface, would probably have thought that the end of a man who departed from life surrounded by every earthly pleasure must have been honourable, yet, in truth, sin—gild and bedizen the outside as you will—sin is ever a coffin—the coffin of the soul; and in this coffin he would have been enclosed, without the possibility of a rising.

Happily a change came over the Prodigal before it was too late. His heart was lonely and desolate, like a home that had been pillaged and wasted by war; yet amidst the cold ashes one little spark remained: he remembered his father's house; he remembered its peace, its abundance, and the kindness that reigned throughout; and the faces of the well-known " hired servants" passed before him in imagination, reflecting, in their calm contentedness, that more noble and tender look which the master of the household carried with him wherever he went.

He remembered these things, and they came to him the more strongly because of the very dreariness of his solitude, just as sweet sounds are louder in the deep stillness of the night, and lights are more brilliant in a chamber encompassed by a surrounding darkness. In the distant past he saw the happiness and purity he had left; in the close present he felt himself more miserable and vile than the swine that he was feeding. The delusion had burst—" he returned to himself."

Returning to himself. How simple and how wonderfully expressive are these words of the parable! What a force of truth they contain! The more remarkable because it is not the language of a poet or an orator, where some allowance may be made for the sake of effect; it is the description of penitence drawn by Jesus Christ Himself. A return to a place means that there has been a departure beforehand; for we cannot come back unless we have first gone away. If, then, a penitent is a man who has come back to himself, a sinner must be a man who has, in some sense, gone away from himself. Herein lies a deep truth which will receive some light from a familiar way of speaking amongst ourselves. Some of you, no doubt, have seen persons out of their mind, either from that dreadful malady insanity, or from the delirium of a fever. Now what is the peculiar character of this state? Is it not that the diseased brain seems to make everything else around diseased also? The poor man, lying perhaps on a scanty bed in a wretched hovel, thinks he is in a palace, and orders everyone about as if he were a monarch. If the room is dark, he says that his eyes are dazzled by the garish light, and he calls for the curtain to be drawn down; if the room is light, he calls for candles; if he is shivering with cold, he asks for the heavy clothes to be removed; and if great drops of perspiration are starting and welling out from every pore of his skin, he calls for more fire. What is most painful of all, he often, with an air of insufferable loathing, pushes away the gentle caress of the wife and child who are naturally most dear to him, and wants to press to his heart strangers whom he has never even seen before. In body and soul he is substantially the same man that he was formerly; still he thinks, talks, and acts as though some evil spirit had changed him into another being. How do we speak of such a one? The wife weeps, and says, "It is my own husband; I know his look, and his voice, and his touch; but, alas, *he is out of his mind!*" Not out of his flesh, nor his soul, but out of *his mind.* He has left his reason, he has left his memory, he has left his affection; they seem dead; and a false reason, a false memory, a false affection, have come in their place. Now mark what happens when the terrible cloud is passing off; as he changes, so all things around change to him. The opposites come right; the phantoms that he saw in the invisible air give way to the well-known figure and voice of his friends; he looks calmly at them, and at himself; the mist is gone; the light of sense breaks quietly within him, and there is a glad cry from those who are around:

"Thank God!" they exclaim; "thank God, he has *come to himself* again!" What makes the wonderful difference in these two states? This: the man was said to have been away from his true self when disease led him to act unlike a rational being, unlike what nature intended him to be; when reason came back, the true *self* returned also. Now man, as you know, is not made only to use his body and his reason; he is *made for God*. To love God, to serve God, to adore God; this is the end of man. In God alone will he find his centre; in God alone will he find the law which will harmonise his whole being. In other words, man can only be what he ought to be by cleaving to God as his very life of life, and heart of heart, and soul of soul. What is this but saying, that the highest and truest self of every man is to be found only *in God?* Forsake God, and you forsake *yourself;* come back to God, and you *return to yourself.* Now, you forsake God by sinning. Sin is that horrible soul-madness, which changes good into evil, and evil into good. Sin makes the poor vanishing things of this world to appear as solid as if they were eternal; and it makes the sweet yoke of Christ feel intolerable. Sin makes the devil appear your friend, and God, who is your most loving Father, appear your enemy. Sin deceives you about the being who is closest to you of all others; it *hoodwinks you about your own self;* so that you are utterly deceived about your own character and the actual condition in which you stand before God. It is only when your eyes open to the sad delusion in which you are living; it is only when you begin accurately to compare earth with heaven, the pleasures of sin with the tremendousness of eternity; it is only when you begin to feel something of that famine of the heart which grace and conscience produce; it is only when you get a true though imperfect glimpse of the real foulness, blackness, poison, and diabolic ungratefulness of your own soul in forsaking God,—it is only then that you begin, like the Prodigal, to return to yourself.

We know that the Prodigal's repentance was sincere, and it is well to observe some of the signs; for as we are deceived by sin in many other things, so we may mistake a false for a real repentance.

For a real repentance it is absolutely necessary that we should be honest with our own selves. If we begin by being dishonest with ourselves, how can we expect to be honest with God? Look at the Prodigal!—he was at last straightforward, however he may have cheated himself before. He looked his position in the face. What was the real, naked truth? He was a feeder of swine on another man's farm. Well, he did not try and imagine that he was in a situation of high honour, and upon his own estate. He was in rags; he did not boast of his purple and fine linen. He was a beggar; he did not play the master. He was fainting from hunger; he did not put on a lying smile, and profess that he was well fed. He was the son of a noble father; but ungrateful, rebellious, and wasteful. He confessed it, and said it would be an undeserved favour if he were to be allowed to take his place with the hired servants of the household. Who can doubt but that this searching examination of the real state of the case was painful? Who can doubt but that many an agonising sigh burst forth from his bruised spirit? Who can doubt but that many tears were counted by the Angels as they watched with holy eagerness the change that was at work within him? So it must ever be. When a disease has penetrated to the very marrow, the touch of the probe, and the cutting of the knife, and the burning of the cautery are painful; but how is the diseased part to be laid open and healed without pain? The sick man does not want to be flattered and soothed: he wants to be cured.

There are some here present, I have no doubt, who are uneasy at their condition; they know that all is not peace within, although they try and fancy the contrary. Now and then, when moved by the words of a preacher, or by some serious event — the death of a friend or sudden loss of property—they make an effort to look in at their hearts. But O, what anxiety there is not to search too deeply! They take a hasty peep through a

Signs of Repentance. 67

small pin's-hole which they prick in that dense curtain which has so long hung in filthy and heavy folds before their conscience, and then, with a very shallow sigh, they draw back again, and leave that thick curtain as it was before. It has been peeped through, and rustled a little bit, but not honestly lifted up to the ceiling. What tricks do men play upon themselves under the name of self-examination! What excuses do they not find for calling sin by other names than sin! If they are passionate, they say it is their nature, for that they were born with an irritable temper, and they cannot help it; if they are idle, they say that they are not able to do much, and that energy is not their strong point; if they go into deliberate temptation, they excuse themselves by pleading that it was an accident; if they are neglectful of devotion, they say that their mind is overburdened with necessary cares; if a Confessor, out of real kindness, puts one or two questions, which, if truly answered, would detect some serious hidden fault, the root of numerous others, he is thought severe, and forsaken for another, who is less particular. Thus in a thousand ways do persons escape the only kind of self-inspection which can lead to a thorough repentance. Of what avail will it be for persons to say that they want to alter their life, if they refuse to take the necessary means? " Prove me, O God, and know my heart; examine me, and know my paths" (Ps. cxxxviii. 23). This was the cry of David. He distrusted his own examination; for he knew how blind he might be, and how partial; so he bares his heart, and beseeches God, who "searcheth the hearts and reins," to do for him what he could not do for himself—to unravel, thread by thread, the network of deceit in which his soul had become entangled, and to pour a flood of light into its furthest corners. And you, how do you act? You are afraid of the judgment of a friend, however true; you start back from the probing of a priest, however gently and skilfully it may be done; you will let no one look into that heart of yours—no, not even yourself, for you shrink from knowing the real extent of the evil which you more than suspect is there.

Are there any persons present who feel an inward stirring in their conscience, moving them to make that examination which they know must be made, if they are to be saved? Are there any here who have delayed coming to confession because they have not, for a long time, had the courage to call up their souls to the bar of their own conscience, misty and blear-eyed as that must be, and to demand an account of the past? If such there be here present, whilst I pity you with my whole heart, I must warn you with my whole force. You say that your soul's history for a long time, perhaps for years, is such a tangled tissue of deliberate sins, of infirmities, of neglects, of bad desires, words, and actions, that you do not know where or how to begin. To search into your past life, you say, is like looking into a dark labyrinth. You feel giddy and oppressed with the very idea of groping along, step by step, through such a series of chambers, one opening into another, and in each a skeleton, which is to be fearlessly handled, measured, and brought out into the light, as every past sin must be when we discover its existence. Be not, however, deceived. Half the task is done when you have honestly determined to do it. God is merciful, and does not require you to perform impossibilities. He does not stand at your side like a stern tyrant, checking off your account of the past with a terribly calm accuracy, and contrasting it with the picture which your life presents to His all-seeing eye. He only asks you to do the best you can, with the help of your memory, such as it is; and with the light of grace, such as you possess. What will you gain by further delay? Will the past, which grows every instant, dwindle down to a more manageable shape as time goes on? Will it be easier to see at the end of another year into that dim distance, which becomes dimmer and dimmer as you depart the farther from it? Who knows whether you will have that future? "The Son of Man cometh at an hour when *you think not;*" and it will be too late then to seize hurriedly the lamp, in order to examine into the slavery and degradation of your soul, when you are summoned to stand before Him, in order to give an account of all things done in the body, and this without the possibility of concealment or evasion.

The trouble of examining into their lives is one reason why men so often put off the duty. There is also another: the revelations, which this inquiry brings to light, are deeply humiliating to their vanity. A course of sin is a course of selfishness, and a course of selfishness is a course of vanity; for all self-pleasing is a form of idolatry. The vengeance of the passionate, the impurity of the lustful, the jealousy of the envious, are all sacrifices, foul as they are, which men make on the altar of self, and it is very hard to be doing all this without admiring that same self; for there is no worship without admiration, even though the idol be a painted bit of clay, or a decrepit ape, or a slimy serpent. Every sinner, then, admires and loves himself to an immoderate degree, and to his own incense he adds that which floats up from friends, flatterers, or the world at large. But a real examination of himself destroys all this illusion; he sees the fine gold turn out to be dross. The wax and paint and tinsel, in which his imaginary self was encased, drop off, and he beholds beneath but a poor specimen of a man and a still poorer specimen of a Christian. Now this is intensely mortifying, and no wonder that so many try every means to put off the day of exposure.

Is there not also another cause why we all hang back so reluctantly from the process? We must be a little more searching in our inquiry, and we shall find out the reason. When the sinner declares that he would repent now, but for the trouble of the task, he tells part of the truth; when he complains of the humiliation of beholding his own vileness, he tells another part. Is there not, however, something else lurking behind, something which is at the bottom of all this reluctance, something without which the examination of conscience, and self-disgust, would be as useless as the tossing of a ship in harbour would be towards speeding her on her course? If she only heaves to and fro at anchor, although she were to continue this motion for ages, she would never be any nearer to the port for which she is destined. Agitation alone is not progress. The Prodigal was in earnest. As he gazed on his own misery, the sense of all his folly and degradation swelled strong in his heart and passed not unfruitfully away; it took shape, it increased in power, it found a voice; a cry, mighty, sincere, victorious, came from the depth of his soul: "I will arise"—"I will arise and go to my Father."

My fellow-sinners, you who are still delaying your repentance, tell me what the secret of this lingering is? Is it *only* the task of examination, is it *only* the shame of confession, is it *only* the fear of seeing yourselves as you really are—is it only this which keeps you back? Is not the hardest difficulty something else? Is it not that you have not yet made up your minds to go on to another step? You are ready to say, "I will look into my heart without flinching. I do not object to tell all I know in the tribunal of penance, without evasion or concealment; but" (O that terrible "but"!) "I am not prepared at present to say with the

Prodigal, 'I will *arise.*'" The resolution, then, to amend has not yet come up, mature and firm, out of the depths of your will; you dare not pledge yourself even to make a determined attempt.

If this be a motive acting upon anyone's mind, the sooner it is detected, the better; the sooner it is grappled with, the better; for the cowardice will increase, instead of diminish, by hesitation; and until you intend to make the resolution of amendment, all else will be vain. You may weep from remorse until your cheeks are furrowed with your tears; you may go over the whole earth, burdening the air with your lamentations; you may confess repeatedly, and tell every sin with the utmost exactness. All will be useless, unless you resolve to give up, as well as to bemoan, your sins; you will remain in them, unforgiven, and growing more fixed in your habits.

O God, merciful and patient, who canst melt the stoniest heart, and give the strength of a giant to the weakest of sinners; have pity on Thy timid, unstable, irresolute children; show them how blessed, how easy it is for all who have strayed, like the Prodigal, from their Father's home, to repent thoroughly like him, if they will only pray for Thy grace with trustful hearts, and follow whithersoever Thy hand shall lead them. "Ask, and ye *shall* receive." "Seek, and ye *shall* find." "Draw nigh to God, and He will draw nigh to you. Cleanse your hands, O ye sinners, and purify your hearts, ye double-minded. Be afflicted, and mourn, and weep: let your laughter be turned into mourning, and your joy into sorrow. Be humbled in the sight of the Lord, and He will exalt you" (James iv. 8-10). "Seek the Lord while He may be found; call upon Him while He is near" (Is. lv. 6).

Why do you hesitate for a moment? Your great enemy, vampire-like, is on the one side, encouraging you to lie still where you are. He is using every art to fan you noiselessly to sleep; he is stupefying your conscience more and more, until all movement will be gone. On the other side, your God is calling to you, as to Lazarus, to come forth from your iniquity.

Yes; Jesus is listening eagerly for the answer. He is bending over your soul's grave; He is holding out to you that crucified right hand, and imploring you to grasp it now; at once, and firmly. Refuse it not: be generous to Him, and merciful to yourselves. "Behold, now is the acceptable time: behold, now is the day of salvation" (2 Cor. vi. 2). "I am the Lord thy God, *who take thee by the hand*, and say to thee, Fear not; I have helped thee, saith the Lord. Fear not, thou worm of Jacob; thou that art dead of Israel, I have helped thee, saith the Lord, and thy Redeemer, the Holy One of Israel" (Is. xli. 13).

V.

HUMILITY AND SINCERITY.

"I will arise and will go to my father, and say to him, Father, I have sinned against heaven and before thee: I am no more worthy to be called thy son." *Luke* xv. 18.

That word "arise," simple as it is in itself, is full of meaning. A man is said to arise when, after having been cast down to the ground, so that he and the earth are as one, he gathers up his limbs and stands upright. Before, he was of the earth, earthy, lying on the ground as if he were its captive; when he arises, he stands upon its surface as on a footstool, and his face looks upward towards the lofty heavens. Whilst down upon the ground, he has little power to defend himself; the sun's hot rays and the pitiless storm beat upon him at their will; and creatures far inferior to himself can violently trample upon, or crawl slowly over, him. But when he springs up, he can fly to some refuge for shelter; or he can do battle with his enemies, face to face and foot to foot. Now we may truly say of all sin, that it takes and throws a man's soul upon the earth. However bright that soul may have been an instant before mortal sin was committed, it is by that act dragged down as with the clutch of a giant; it is covered with the dust and stain of pollution; it is taken off its feet and stripped of its spiritual armour; it lies helpless and degraded in the territory of its chief enemy; it is walked over and trampled upon by an ever-increasing train of rebellious thoughts, desires, and passions. Evil spirits make sport of and swarm around it, as the Philistines mocked Samson of old when they had tied him fast with cords and plucked out both his eyes.

If this be one effect of sin, the determination to repent must be the corresponding opposite. Whoever says, "I will arise," does in reality say, " I will leave my weakness, and be strong; I will leave my slavery, and be free; I will leave the uncleanness I have contracted, and be clean; no longer will I suffer wicked demons, the ministers of Satan, to triumph over and mock me; I will walk with God, and be a companion of the good Angels, who—unseen though they be—are ever around the path of the penitent."

The word "arise" also suggests to our mind the idea of an awakening from sleep. In the darkness of the night men sleep: their limbs move not, and their mind is but half-conscious. The sleeper, when awake, may be capable of noble deeds: he may be a Newton, who can discover the wonderful laws of Nature; he may be a statesman, able to influence the fate of mighty nations; he may be a poet, whose lays will become household words; or a painter, whose skill will attract thousands from distant parts of the globe; or he may be a warrior, whose right arm, with its trusty blade, can scatter death by its sweep. The sleeper may be any or all these characters; but who could suppose it, seeing him only in a state of slumber? As we bend over the closed eyelids and silent form, what can seem to us more powerless? for sleep, like death, is a great leveller of persons. The great and little, the rich and poor, the learned and dull, are all confounded together in the same uniform stillness: there is no work going on in slumber. But wait awhile—wait till the darkness rolls away, and the sunlight flashes through the room; wait till each man's consciousness comes back; wait till his brain is ready to start again the wonderful machinery of thought; wait till the various muscles of the body obey the call of the will—then the man arises, and his characteristic forces begin to show their power.

So it is with the spiritual sleep and the spiritual arising. Sin encloses the soul in thick darkness—a darkness, like that of Egypt, "that may be felt." The countenance of God is veiled before the sinner: he does not behold—or at most sees very dimly—even the attributes of God; he has but poor thoughts about the holiness of God, that holiness which cannot bear the slightest spot of iniquity. He forgets the all-embracing presence of God, and remembers not that an all-searching Eye is everywhere, by day or night, piercing with its glance into the most secret recesses of the soul. He forgets that everywhere, too, is the hand of God supporting all things, even the sinner himself, who abuses the gifts of God, so as with them to resist God Himself. There is a thick mist concealing the loveliness of a holy life, and shrouding the glory that awaits the faithful in heaven. There is darkness hiding the terrible "two-edged sword"—the wrath of God—which ever hangs, as though suspended by a hair, over the sinner; there is darkness covering over, in order to deceive us, the fiery abyss of hell. So, also, whilst he continues in his iniquity, the soul of the sinner is paralysed, and can do no work worthy of a redeemed soul; it can acquire no merit; it cannot advance an inch heavenward. Move it does; for a sinner who does not repent *must* be going on; but the movement is down, down, instead of up; and farther into darkness and sleep, instead of being a progress in the contrary direction. When, therefore, a sinner says sincerely, "I will arise," it is saying, in other words, "I will go into the kingdom of light; I will follow the commandment of the Lord, which is the path of the just, and which, as 'a shining light, goeth forwards and increaseth even to the perfect day' (Prov. iv. 18). I will no longer follow a confused and blind conscience—no longer follow him whose name is well called the Prince of Darkness, for his snares and abode are alike dark; but I will follow Him who is ever Light of Light, whether He be in the rude manger at Bethlehem, or on Mount Tabor, where His countenance shone like the sun; whether He be upon the Cross, crying out, 'My God, My God, why hast Thou forsaken Me?' or seated on His throne, as He is now, surrounded ever by myriads of angels. I will follow that Jesus, Whose word, Whose grace, Whose crown, Whose city, is all light: 'The city hath no need of the sun nor of the moon to shine in it; for the glory of God hath enlightened it, and the Lamb is the light thereof'" (Apoc. xxi. 23).

There is a little word to which I must now direct your attention; because, unless its force be well understood, you may easily fall into the error of confounding a false with a true repentance. That little word is one of which the babe knows the meaning before it can speak—a word which we never forget, and which we all love a great deal too much. I mean the word "I." When the Prodigal cried out, "*I* will arise," he really meant what he said. Is it true that *we* always mean what the Prodigal meant, when *we* use the same words? I fear not; nay, I am sure not; for if we did, we should not fail so often to bring forth "fruits worthy of repentance." Now what is the full force of that word "I"?—*I* is myself, my very self. It signifies my whole being. When the word "arise" is used of the body, and a man says, "I will arise," he does not mean that one foot only shall be lifted up, or a hand, or the head. He means that the complete body with all its several members shall move, and stand up erect. In the same way, when we speak of the rising up of the soul from sin, we do not mean that one or two faculties only shall arise—the reason, for instance, or the imagination—but that the heart, reason, imagination, and will shall *all* arise; for it is these together that make up that mysterious unity of the soul called "I."

Whoever, therefore, intends to repent must bear in mind that, just as moving a foot or a hand, and nothing else, will leave the body on the ground, so, in a similar manner, a partial moving of the soul will leave the soul just where it was before, in the bondage of sin and death. Nor can any contrary belief of yours alter the fact. A dreaming or an insane person may easily fancy that he is up and walking, when the bystanders — who are neither dreaming nor insane — know perfectly well that the man is still stretched full length on his bed, tossing to and fro, but not off the bed, although perhaps a small portion of his body may be outside the clothes. Nor does any delusion to the contrary, on his side, change the real state of the case. With regard to repentance, it must be observed that a mere wish to forsake sin is not enough. The most hardened sinners have these wishes, and die in their sins. We see the uselessness of mere wishes in worldly matters, and call it folly. A hungry man may wish that he had bread; a slothful man may wish that he had the carriages and horses that sweep past him; and so on. But what are wishes like these worth? surely, not much. They are arrows fixed on a bow-string which is never pulled; they are beatings of the air, which strike no adversary. Do not confound wishes to repent, of this kind, with a *will* to repent. You have seen a lake rippled slightly by the breeze; at first, you would fancy that the whole body of water was going to roll on to the land. You soon find that there is no peril: you may safely stand a yard from the edge for an entire day if you choose; the lake itself no more advances than a man walks because he has a fit of shivering. Now look at a tide: there you see ripples too; but the ripples are waves, and the waves march on, so that if you stand long where you are, you will be swept away. That is just the difference between a mere *wish* to repent, and a *real intention :* the one is only a surface-ripple of the mind; the other is the soul rising up, and moving on with a victorious will to a real change of conduct.

Again, a man cannot be said to have arisen from sin when he is unable, through circumstances, to commit it. Exterior sins cannot be committed unless the means are at hand. A drunkard cannot be intoxicated if no alcoholic liquor is to be obtained; a thief cannot steal unless there is property within the reach of his fingers; a calumniator cannot blacken a character if there is no character to be blackened. Want of opportunity to sin is not repentance. In one sense, a man may be said to have risen from a sin, when, through some cause or other, he has been removed from the means of actually committing it. But what if his heart is always in that direction? What if his imagination is accustomed to bring up before its phantasy the pleasures of former sins, and to feed gloatingly upon the idea? What if he and his favourite sin are separated by time and place only, the unholy union being as strong as ever? Such a person cannot say, "I have arisen," or "I will arise;" for the heart, which is the main part of a man's true self, is still clinging to the iniquity which he professes to have abandoned. There is no real arising of the soul, unless we leave the known occasion of sin.

When the Prodigal came to a sense of his misery, and saw that he was nearly perishing with hunger, when he thought also deeply and seriously of the sin he had committed, the next step was to leave at once the country where he had fallen into such a terrible snare. He did not stop lingering in memory over the past; he did not keep recalling the looks and dangerous attractions of his evil companions. He saw plainly that this "far country" had been to him, whatever it may have been to others, a pit only, a prison, and a wilderness. So he started back at once on his way home. No fear of being laughed at, no threats, no dread of the hardships he would have to encounter, held him back. The arch-fowler had for a long time kept him in his meshes. Why should he linger any longer to have his pinions still more tightly bound, and his once-bright feathers draggled still more in the mire?

Learn from the Prodigal to break off instantly from all places, all company, and all employments or pleasures which are necessarily injurious to your soul. If the Prodigal had not gone right away from the "far country" as soon as he began to repent, he might never have left it at all; and then, of what use would have been his sorrow, of what use his misery, of what use his words, "I will arise"? They would have witnessed against him, because they would prove how strongly he had been moved by the Spirit of God, but they would have done nothing for his escape. Whoever says, "I will arise," is only bringing fresh condemnation upon himself if he remains of his own accord in the midst of temptations, which must sooner or later bring him down again into the same pit from which he has for a short time escaped. Do not you, in the Lord's Prayer, say daily, "Lead us not into temptation"? Do not you, every time you go to confession, declare that you "resolve to avoid the *occasions* of sin"? What should we think of a person who, after having, by much exertion, been rescued from a watery grave, should go and swim close round the edge of the eddy that had before sucked him in, or sucked in others like himself? What should we think of a person who, after having once been robbed and nearly beaten to death, should go and sleep at the entrance of the very forest from which the bandits came?

When, therefore, you have found out that certain persons are most dangerous to your peace of mind, or your sense of justice, or your modesty, avoid them; although they coax you with all their fascinating skill, although they jeer you as cleverly as they can, although they try to alarm you with false fears, never mind; tell them that you value the grace of God more than their esteem; tell them that you are not going to throw away, to please them, the experience you have bought so dearly. However attractive these temptations may be, let them be to you what the "far country," the famine, and the swine-tending were to the Prodigal—things to be fled from, if you mean to go securely to your long-abandoned home and your Father.

"Father," said the Prodigal, "I have *sinned* against heaven and before thee." "*I have sinned.*" Mark that word well; for much of our unfruitful penitence results from our failing to acknowledge, as we ought, the real nature of our conduct. Although a little reflection will show us that we have sinned, how anxious we are to call our conduct by some gentler name! A person commits some grievous offence against the sixth commandment, ruining his own purity, and perhaps destroying for ever the innocence of another. How is this iniquity too often spoken of? It is called a *misfortune!* as if the sin were one of those accidents which may happen to any one against his will. How often is some sin spoken of as if it were an absolute necessity!

"I told a great falsehood—I gave way to a furious passion—I suspected somebody without cause—I provoked another to swear—I cursed bitterly my children; *but I could not help it;* I was obliged to do these things." Such is the way in which men talk. They will call their conduct anything you like, except just that which it really is—a sin.

How fond, also, we are of throwing all or the chief blame of our actions upon other persons! Instead of confessing, "*I* have sinned," we only attack others, and say, "*They* have sinned." Mass is neglected; and what is the common excuse? "My husband, or my wife, was in a bad temper, or my children were troublesome;" "I went to a place dangerous to my soul, but a friend treated me;" "I drank more than I ought, but it was at a christening, or a wedding, or a funeral." The blame is cast upon anybody rather than ourselves.

If this is all our repentance, it can be of little worth; it is not confession, but self-defence; it is justification, not sorrow. How is it possible to have real penitence, when the chief aim of our mind is not to see our guilt? The more you try to lessen your own fault, the less must be your contrition; for we are sorry for a sin just in proportion as we acknowledge that we are guilty and without excuse.

The Prodigal could have suggested much

in his own defence. He might have said, "I was young and thoughtless, and I had not acquired the habit of reflection; I had money in abundance, and was brought up in refinement; I wished, with a most natural curiosity, to see the world, and, unfortunately, I fell in with bad associates." The Prodigal, however, is blind and dumb to such vain excuses; all that he can see is, heaven and his father outraged, and himself the man who has done this wrong. The prophet Nathan, on a memorable occasion, charging king David with grievous iniquities, said to him, "*Thou* art the man." The Prodigal was his own Nathan, and said to himself in the full bitterness of his soul, "I—I and no other have sinned against heaven and before thee. I, who ought to have known better. I, who have had so many graces poured upon me. I, who have had every inducement to be good. I, who have had such prosperity, such health, such strength, given me in order to serve my God well. *I* am that ungrateful son who has, scorpion-like, turned upon and stung my own father's heart to the quick. I have sinned, and am no more worthy to be called *thy son*. Call me, if thou wilt, thy disgrace; call me thy misery; call me thy unnatural rebel; call me thy enemy. Such words, I admit, are true to the letter; but to be called still thy *son*, O, of that I am utterly unworthy!"

What was the thought which so pierced the Prodigal's soul? What was it that not only struck it, as a hammer may strike a rock, but also in the striking brought forth, like the rod of Moses, such a gush of real sorrow, such a torrent of tender humiliation? It was the remembrance of his father. The Prodigal knew well that he had sinned against his own reason—against his conscience; he knew that he had broken the moral law. But that which wounded him most was the inward pang of having offended his father. The sins he had committed were sad enough in their effects upon himself, sad enough as violations of what was due to the law of right that should govern every reasonable soul; but in every sin the Prodigal saw that he had shot an arrow against his father's heart. "I have sinned," he cried, but the cry went on farther, "against heaven and *before thee.*" In like manner, if you desire to have the Prodigal's repentance, you must learn to look at sin as he did. There is a way of saying, "I have sinned," which has none of this spirit in it. There are men who admit that they have done wrong, because they are frank and truth-telling; they see it plainly by the force of common sense and common honesty; and yet there is no sorrow in their confession; there is truth without contrition. There are others who say, "I have sinned," and are actually proud of being humble enough to confess what cannot be denied without falsehood. There are others who say, "I have sinned," and who by habit are so used to sinning that they think little of it *as guilt;* they are perhaps ashamed of it, as a weakness or a stupidity, just as a person may be ashamed of some breach of polite manners; others are not ashamed at all, but have come to regard sin as something natural and to be expected. Like the diseases that are generally looked for in childhood, sins are matters to be lamented, but, still, matters of course—phenomena of human nature.

The true penitent, on the contrary, never forgets the real character of sin. The misery, the disgrace, the thousand other effects of sin, he knows as well as anyone else; but the one thing which brings his head down to the dust, the one thing which makes him, like David, water his couch with tears, is the thought that all this has been done by a son against a most tender father. In sin he beholds not only a breaking of the law of God, but a cruelty, an unnatural blow aimed parricidally against God Himself. "I have sinned against heaven and *before Thee;*" "to Thee alone have I sinned," —Thee, my God and my All.

Wormwood as this thought is to the penitent sinner, and deeply as it goes into his spirit, who would wish to escape from it? Who would wish for penitence without this writhing of the heart? Who would wish for the mere dry logic of self-conviction, without the keener thrill that springs from the feeling that we have sinned against our Father?

Yet even here there is a balm; the arrow carries within it a hidden strength, pouring oil into the very wound which it opens. For if the thought that we have grieved our heavenly Father increases our sorrow, is there not another thought which lifts up the heart that is bruised? is there not a trembling yet hopeful spirit poured into our soul? is it not cast down in order that it may look up? He that cries out, "I have sinned against my Father," is he not the same who also says, "I will arise and go to my Father"? Yes; thanks be to God, though we have sinned, God has not for a moment ceased to be our Father! Behold, then, a great encouragement! behold a ray of joy! O sinner, be not dismayed; if thou art penitent, thou art *already going to thy Father*. If the way is thorny—if clouds overshadow thy path—if the devil tries to weary thee out, remember to cry aloud in reply, "What do I care for these difficulties? I am going to my Father; not to my Creator only, not to my future Judge only, but to my Father, who will not disown a repentant child. Has He not said by His prophet, "As a father hath compassion on his own children, so hath the Lord compassion on them that fear Him" (Ps. cii. 13). Has not Jesus Christ said with His own lips, "Him that cometh to Me, I will *not* cast out"? (John vi. 37.)

VI.

MERCY AND TRUST.

"Rising up, he came to his father; and when he was yet a great way off, his father saw him, and was moved with compassion, and running to him, fell on his neck and kissed him." *Luke* xv. 20.

STRANGE as it may sound, it is nevertheless true that many who did not fear to brave the anger of God at the moment when they committed sin, begin to dread it most when they are anxious to repent. They were rash, blind, and venturesome when they ought to have been wise, vigilant, and fearful; and now, when they ought to be trustful, they are cast down with alarm. Their eyes being opened, they are horrified to find where sin has led them; into what defilement, into what a terrible network of evil. They look at the blackness of their hearts, at the awful closeness of hell, and at the distance they have gone from holiness, until they can see scarcely anything else. As formerly they were beguiled and made drunk by the intoxication of sin, so that they were regardless of God's anger, now they are so overpowered by the thought of His vengeance that they forget or underrate His mercy. To a man in a panic in the night-time, everything is alarming; and so it is with those whom I am describing. Heaven and earth seem nothing but one great court of assize, in which they stand as though they were the only criminals in the world. Everywhere their soul hears nothing but the roll of the thunder of divine justice; everywhere the avenging sword seems to turn and flash. "Whither shall I go from Thy spirit, or whither shall I fly from Thy face?" is their constant inward cry. Anxious as they are to reform, there appears so little hope in the task that they are almost tempted to despair. They know well that it will cost them much suffering to break off from their many evil ways, and nothing but suffering is in view. They loathe themselves; they are depressed by the gloom with which the devil takes care to fill their imagination, and they dare not look up to God for fear of being withered by His wrathful eye. Are some of you saying, in the bitterness of your heart, "That is my case, or something like it; I want to be good, but I am crushed and weighed down by anxiety, and sadness, and distrust"? I invite you then to watch the Prodigal on his return, and observe how he was treated. You have followed him step by step in his history; you believe that he was for a long time ungrateful, wasteful, and a companion of the wicked. You believe in the reality of his misery, you believe in the pangs of famine which he endured; you have, in thought, watched him gaunt, and ragged, and hungry, envying the lot of the unclean swine, which he tended for a stranger. You believe all this; then believe equally the next page of his career. Dark as his night has been, the morning has at length broken; if the clouds, and the storm, and the desolation once left him dead, like a corpse thrown amongst the rocks by the waves, yet he has found a resurrection.

"He was dead, and is come to life again; was lost, and is found." "The winter is now past, the rain is over and gone; the flowers have appeared in our land."

For you, who are really in earnest about your repentance, and yet are overmuch cast down with fear, the parable of the Prodigal is surely full of consolation. Spoken, as it was, many centuries ago, it is as much meant for you now as if you had been listening to it in the Holy Land, when it came fresh from the lips of your Lord. You have arisen in will from your state of sin, but at present there seems a "great gulf fixed" between you and God. You seem to stand on one side, and the just yet merciful Judge on the other; you wonder if you can pass it; you wonder if He will stretch forth the olive-branch of pardon to you, for the olive-branch at present looks distant. But what are we told about the returning Prodigal? As he journeyed along, ragged and footsore, doubtless he felt the pressure of the solitude; strangers to him might now and then give him water from the wayside well, and speak a kind word; but the sorrow and self-reproach within must have made him feel that all the world was dreary; though repentant, he was alone—alone with his memory, alone with his past sins, alone with his conscience. Nevertheless, he was not so entirely alone as he thought; not so far off from home as he seemed. There was a look fixed upon him in the distance, whose eager gaze was watching for his return with a tenderness beyond the power of any words to express. Who was it that was straining his very eyeballs to pierce through the dimness of the distance? Who was it that for many a weary day had mounted the lofty watch-tower and scanned the horizon so often in vain? Who was it that had sent messenger upon messenger to reclaim a wanderer? Who was it that yearned to see that stray sheep, no matter in what plight he should come? Who was it that, in spite of the pale haggard face, and the tired dragging of the limbs, and the tattered rags, recognised one that was loved with a love that could not be extinguished, one who had been seen last when in the full beauty and vigour of his youth? Who was it that could not be deceived in that humbly-approaching figure, whom the servants will treat as a stranger, and at whom the once-familiar dogs will bark so suspiciously and savagely? It was the father of the Prodigal. Who else could it be?

"When he was yet a great way off his father saw him and was moved with compassion." The Prodigal saw none but himself; he saw his own misery and sorrow well: but mercy is keen-sighted; mercy sees farther than contrition; so the father saw the son *"when he was a great way off."*

In like manner, your heavenly Father has seen you "when a great way off." He has seen you in various ways. Never for a moment has He lost sight of you. When you sinned and tried to escape His eye, He followed you, and you felt His look, although, perhaps, you did not admit that it was His. Is it not true that often in the midst of your blind passions you have experienced strange stirrings of the heart, that would not be quieted? Have you not hated yourself in secret for your ungratefulness? Have you not, when lying on your bed and perhaps bowed down by sickness, longed to flee from some evil habit which enslaved you? Have you not consented to commit sin with others because you had promised to do so, and yet have prayed that something might happen to prevent you from keeping your word? Have you not often lingered at the entrance of the confessional, half determined to go in, and make your peace with God? Have you not tried to keep your comrades out of sins which you were bold enough to commit yourself, in the hope that you might at least be saved the additional guilt of involving others in ruin? These and a thousand other things were nothing else but inspirations of grace sent to you from God. They were rays of light that found their way into the gloom of your sinful state, and came from your Father's eye; they were the unseen touches of His outstretched hand. O the amazing humility, O the exhaustless patience of God! Why should He watch so anxiously every step of a sinner? Why should He, Who could create millions of worlds full of sinless beings in a moment if He liked, follow, as if with an all-absorbing anxiety, the rebellious ramblings of a worthless sinner? You could not increase the essential happiness of God if you returned to Him a thousand times, and you could not lessen it if you abandoned Him a thousand times. God has worlds full of wonders and beauties of which we know nothing; and yet like a good shepherd, who leaves all to bring back a single sheep, who crosses rivers, and searches into foul caves, and goes down steep precipices, and tears his hands with rescuing his sheep from the brambles, and faces the hungry wolves, so God seems never to rest in His search for one poor insignificant wandering soul. "Who hath wrought and done these things? I, the Lord" (Is. xli. 4).

Often you have been surrounded by an army of temptations, of whose number and force you knew little; you have been hemmed in by a thousand arts of the devil, who has incessantly followed, and laid unseen snares for, your soul; and then something quite unexpected has happened which has released you. This was the mercy of God, Who saw you a great distance off, and made a way for your escape, although at the time you knew not from what quarter the deliverance came. "He hath delivered me from the snare of the hunters" (Ps. xc. 3).

Why, then, should you fear to come near to Him, now that you are anxious to repent? Do you want a proof of His mercy? He has given it already; for whence does this desire of repentance spring? Whence comes this fear of judgment, and this detestation of your former life, but from God? The object of the devil is to lull you into indifference, and the effect of continued sin is to harden your conscience. When a man is dead he ceases to feel. The very fact, therefore, that your soul trembles with awe, and is stirred with sorrow, and draws back in humility from the presence of the holiness of God, this alone proves that God is showing you unspeakable mercy.

You may well exclaim with David, "O my

God, and my *mercy ;*" " my God," therefore
" my *mercy.*" What fuller pledge of love do
you want than this? When Lazarus felt the
thrill of life running through his frame, he
knew that some power not his own had touched
him; and so you may be assured that the fear,
anxiety, and sorrow that are for the moment
casting you down, are nothing else but the
shadow of the hand of God, which is now upon
you, not to smite but to draw you to Himself.
"I will draw them with the bands of love"
(Osee xi. 4).

Do not think that any past sins, however
great, can be an irremovable barrier between you
and God. Long before you were able to commit
even the slightest venial sin, He saw your future
mortal sins, and had compassion and determined to forgive you, if you would but turn to
Him. Pity for you is no sudden thought, no
new feeling with God. Go back in imagination for millions and millions of years, when
there was no being but God in the universe.
He saw you then with an eye of tenderness; for
He saw, in the clearness of His vision, that He

meant to create you. How could it be otherwise? God, Who beholds all things, actual and possible, is *love;* "God *is* love;" and therefore the very same Eye which, looking through eternity, saw in the divine plan the creation of you and every other being, was from eternity the Eye of infinite love. Not only before you sinned, but before you breathed, before an atom of the earth, on which you now tread, existed—before anything was made to image God in creation, *you* were pitied. In the deep silence of the abyss of the solitude of the eternal Trinity, one sound was ever heard—the mystical beat of the fatherly heart of God for those who in after ages were to be His ungrateful but finally repentant sons. "When he was a great way off, his father saw him, and was moved with compassion."

I have taken you back to the time when nothing was created, and when nothing therefore could have sinned. For one moment go back in thought to the time when not only had sin defiled the earth, but when its crowning iniquity was done. Eighteen centuries ago the wonderful and awful mystery of the Crucifixion took place. In front of, and for a vast circuit around, the cross an immense multitude stood; of this multitude not a unit was hidden from the look of Jesus. Through the blinding streams of blood that poured from His thorn-pierced head, His eye of pity found each one out, and by the touching love which it expressed wrestled with each for his conversion. And far beyond the crowd, far beyond Jerusalem, far beyond that age, did the look of the dying Jesus reach. He saw you, each one of you, as distinctly as though you had been as near to the cross as the Blessed Virgin herself, although you were as yet unborn. He saw all the sins into which you would fall; He saw all your future misery and distress, your abandonment of Himself, your betrayal of Him in a thousand ways. This humiliating vision increased the bitterness of the cup He was draining to the dregs. Nevertheless, in the midst of all He had compassion upon you; and as in His divine foreknowledge He beheld your fall, so also by the same foreknowledge He beheld your return, and caught by anticipation, as He was dying, the sweet sound of penitence—"Father, I have sinned against heaven and before Thee, and am not worthy to be called Thy son." The heart of the crucified One therefore rejoiced; for He could say, "This My son was dead, and has come to life again; was lost, and is found."

When we consider what an outrage sin is against the majesty of God, nothing short of a revelation from Him could have convinced us of His tenderness towards the sinner. As the Prodigal came towards his home, doubtless his intention was to have waited in abject humiliation until he was seen by some of the servants. Like the publican, he meant to have stood afar off, beating his breast; how dared he venture to pass the threshold of the home he had despised! He felt that the very domestic animals had more right there than himself, for they, at all events, had never forsaken the hand that fed and caressed them. As he looked up at the outer walls of the mansion, the stones appeared to cry out against him for his ingratitude. The vine and the fig-trees and the pomegranates and the olives had all been faithful, and brought forth fruit as usual; the cattle had trod out the corn and multiplied their kind; but the *son* returned with nothing to show but misery. Yes, there was one thing beneath all, which the father saw although others might not—the bruised heart and the sincere determination to leave his home no more. This it was which changed everything into goodness and beauty and honour. This it was which drew the father's heart so mightily that he would not wait until his son came near. The offence done to his dignity, and the ill-return shown to his affection, were buried in a generous oblivion. The father, as though borne along by an irresistible current of love, did not stop a moment, but "*running*, fell upon his neck and kissed him." The son came along slowly, for he was sad; slowly, for he was doing penance; slowly, because of his sense of unworthiness. The father ran because of the eagerness of his affection and his anxiety to pour balm into the torn heart of his child. What a triumph of love! Truly in a most holy sense love was in this case blind. There was the Prodigal, there was the sinner, squalid and stained with dust from his weary journey. Many would deem it a dishonour to be seen even speaking to such a miserable outcast; society would pass him by in scorn; the proud Pharisees of their day would hardly think him worth denouncing; but the father was blind to all these considerations, he beheld before him nothing but his repentant child. The great depths of his heart heaved as with an earthquake; so that, on reaching his son, he "fell upon his neck and kissed him" as if fainting from the thrill of so much pity and love. Before the best robe and the ring, which he ordered the servants to fetch, had time to arrive, the father had pressed the son to his bosom, so that their hearts might throb together as one; the heart of penitence sinking deep on the heart of forgiveness; trouble resting upon peace, fear upon reassuring mercy; misery and degradation shielded, surrounded, and hidden by the glory and joy of the father's charity. "He fell upon his neck and kissed him;" he fell upon the neck that had been so stubborn and proud; he kissed the lips that had muttered so callously and so selfishly, "Give me the portion of goods that falleth to me, and let me go"—the lips that had been a short time before so polluted by intemperance and lust. He fell upon that neck, for it was now bowed low in humiliation; and he kissed those lips, for they had now sanctified themselves by that precious confession, "I have sinned; I am not now worthy to be called thy son." How real the Prodigal's repentance was, may be seen not only from his conduct before he reached his father, but, if possible, still more strongly afterwards; for he not only declared that he would confess his sin and his ungratefulness, before he knew how mercifully he would be received, but in the very midst of his father's caresses, from beneath that close embrace, there was heard again the same confession. If the father remembered that the Prodigal was his own son, the son also did not forget that, as a prodigal, he had deeply sinned, even though he was now treated as tenderly as if he had been always innocent: "Father, I have sinned against heaven and before thee, and am not *now* worthy to be called thy son."

So let it be with you. Learn to have the whole spirit of the returned Prodigal; his spirit of sorrow, and also his spirit of reverential confidence. Whatever your sins may have been, fear not, as long as you are determined to repent. Jesus sees you with a look of compassion beyond all words; at your homes, at your prayers, in your employments, in the church, His loving eye is ever upon you. Above all, He looks at you with tenderness when you kneel in the tribunal of penance; then you are near to Him; so near, that as He bends over you the Precious Blood drops on your soul. He is nearer still at the altar, where, indeed, He falls upon your neck, and kisses you with an inward embrace, in which He and you are blended together as "one flesh." "I in you, and you in Me." "I to my Beloved, and my Beloved to me. His left hand under my head, and His right hand shall embrace me" (Cant. vi. 3, viii. 2). "As one whom the mother caresseth, so will I comfort you, and you shall be comforted in Jerusalem" (Is. lxvi. 13).

How appropriate, too, is the epithet of "running," as applied to our Blessed Redeemer! When Adam fell, he was instantly consoled by the promise of a Saviour: he had not to wait until the end of a severe penitential life before he heard the prophecy of his restoration (Gen. iii. 15). As soon as it was possible, consistently with the just designs of Perfect Wisdom, the Incarnation so long foretold was effected. Jesus did not wish to delay His Passion; His language was, "How am I straitened until it be accomplished!" "He hath rejoiced as a giant to *run* the way." When we were babes, unconscious that we had been conceived in sin, did He not meet us early with the cleansing waters of Baptism? Did He not then embrace us, and put upon us the robe of righteousness, and give us the kiss of peace, so that we could say, "Abba, Father"? Does He not now constantly come to us, unasked, through the zeal of apostolic men, who burn with His own love for sinners, and are ever on the watch to bring them back towards their true home? Does He not often hasten, in the persons of His priests, to convey the Absolution, and the Viaticum, and the Holy Unction to some poor forlorn creature, who has had the grace to repent on a deathbed, perhaps only a few hours, or even moments, before unconsciousness sets in?

Rejoice, O penitent sinner, for all these mercies; rejoice that "the commiserations of the Lord have not failed; they are new every morning: great is thy faithfulness. The Lord is good to them that hope in Him, to the soul that seeketh Him. The Lord will not cast off for ever; for if He hath cast off, He will also have mercy according to the multitude of His mercies" (Lament. iii. 22).

But whilst you rejoice, exclaiming with the Psalmist, "I will praise Thee for ever because Thou hast done it," forget not that you are utterly undeserving of such mercy: say, even to your last breath, nay, though, like St. Stephen, you should behold the heavens opening to welcome you to your Father's home, after wandering in the far-off land of this earth, made still more distant from that home by your sins,—say always, and with your whole heart, "Father, I have sinned against heaven and before Thee, and am no more worthy to be called Thy son."

THE SOWER.

I.

THE SOWER: HIS PERSON AND OFFICE.

"Behold, the sower went forth to sow." *Matthew* xiii. 3.

THE Gospel-narrative has not only handed down to us the words of our Divine Lord, when He uttered the parable of the Sower, but it has also given us an idea of the circumstances under which He spoke. And I need not say that if we treasure up the truths of Jesus Christ as we ought, we shall feel an intense delight in those minute details which bring vividly before us the place and surroundings of our Lord's address.

We may say, in truth, that fervent love knows nothing of trifles: everything which refers to its beloved,—place, words, tone of voice, looks, actions,—all are precious. Love delights in turning the past into a present; it spells out every syllable that speaks of the beloved object, and seizes with eagerness everything which brings before it more clearly the person in whom it delights. Let us try, then, to imagine for a moment the circumstances under which our Lord spoke.

Having left His modest home, He made His way towards the Sea of Tiberias; perhaps He went there for solitude, wishing for no voice to speak to Him but the murmur of the waves upon the shore—those waves which, sometimes calm, sometimes turbulent, were no unapt image of the fickleness of those whom He had come to save. Perhaps He went forth to pray for the Gentiles, having, as an ancient Father observes, left His home, which was a figure of the House of Israel, for that wider ocean of humanity, the nation of the Gentiles. However this may be, His peaceful solitude was soon broken. He Who was the Creator of the world could not sit for a little while upon the sea-shore without being disturbed. This is only one of numberless instances which show to us that the Son of Man, although Lord of all things, had nothing of His own. The cradle of His birth was not His own; He had no house which He claimed as His own; His winding-sheet and grave were borrowed. So here again, as soon as He had sat down, possibly weary with journeying, His quiet is invaded. Groups of all classes gather round Him; some from curiosity, some hoping for a miracle, others from real earnestness. By degrees the numbers grew so large that His Divine Person was pressed upon on all sides; His freedom was impeded; the Son of Man was lost in the over-eager swarming, and hustling of a crowd. So at length He entered into a boat and pushed off a little into the sea. Then, being seated, as a sign of His royalty, —seated too in that memorable boat which, as owned by Peter, was a significant emblem and prophecy of the future Catholic Church,—Jesus spoke. Before Him were the multitudes ranged, row behind row,—men, women, and children, Jews and Pagans, rich and poor, His enemies and His disciples. All eyes were fixed upon

Jesus, and the eyes of Jesus were reading the interiors of all. Not a thought was there in the minds of that vast multitude which was hidden from Him; every fibre of each man's life was laid bare before Him; all their separate histories, from their creation to that moment; the yet unborn future of each, the eternal fate of each—all these things were open to the glance of the Son of Man. He faced the people, and they stood before Him, with only a slip of rippling water between them both; between God and His creatures; between the Shepherd and His sheep; between holiness and sin; truth and ignorance; the Redeemer and those whom He came to redeem; the future Judge and those who were ere long to stand before His unerring tribunal. The scene itself was a parable; for the dry sandy shore might well represent the barren land of this our exile, separated by the ebbing and flowing of the hours of life from "Him that sitteth on the throne, Who liveth for ever and ever" (Apoc. iv. 9).

Let us now consider the opening words of the parable. "Behold, the sower went forth to sow." There are three distinct points to be noticed in this declaration:— the person and character of him who went forth, "the sower;" — the manner in which he began his work, by "going forth;"— and the object of his going forth, "to sow." Knowing, as we do, that our Lord always intended to convey some important spiritual truth under the homeliest of His figures of speech, we should have been prepared, even without His own explicit declaration, to have conjectured that the sower was no ordinary dispenser of divine seed. From the fall of Adam there had been a long series of men whose especial office was to act as messengers from God, as fellow-workers with Him in that celestial husbandry of which the world in its darkest days was never utterly deprived. The greatest, however, of these sowers, the Patriarchs and Prophets of old, were but men: and the seed which they dropped was mightier than themselves. Notwithstanding their inspiration and wonder-working powers, they were not always able to penetrate the full meaning of their own ministry;

they were servants, not masters; they went forth only to pass away; they were but the faintly-projected shadows of One Who alone truly bears that name of "Sower," which is applicable to them solely in a reflected and imperfect sense. The Sower in the parable is One who is emphatically deserving of the title in its most exclusive and perfect signification. Just as when there is only one monarch in a kingdom, we say "The King,"—meaning that he has no sharer and no rival in the sovereignty, and that, if there be others who have authority, they derive it wholly from him, and are simply his deputies and servants, the channels through which the King administers his rule, the wires which convey his will to others,—so, in like manner, there is an unmistakable and peculiar force in the phrase, "The Sower." It means that all fruit-giving seed is in that Sower's hand; it means that without Him the earth that is to be sowed can produce nothing good; it means that without Him the best of seed can effect nothing, however abundantly it may be applied to the ground; it means that all others who sow must come from Him, and act under His authority, and that without Him they are as useless as the earth without seed. Before I say one word more, you will all see that "the Sower" in the parable can be no one else but the Son of God Himself. He is indeed the only person who can justly be called "The Sower." In Him is gathered up all life; in Him is all power; from Him springs all fruitfulness; in Him is treasured up all grace; upon Him hangs salvation. The earth, of which the parable speaks, means the souls of men; and the very words, *the Sower*, mark out at once a great fundamental truth; namely, that until God comes, and acts upon the soul, it can do nothing good. What can mere soil do, unless it is sown? Years may roll on by millions; the sun may waste his beams upon it, and the rain and dew may fall upon it perpetually: but without the seed and the sower, it will remain only barren earth. So it is with the souls of men: whatever natural powers they may have, never can they produce the harvest of true wisdom and true goodness, without the help of the Great Sower. The soul of man must remain a corpse until He Who is Life has dropped into it the seed of a divine vitality. Nature cannot produce grace; fallen humanity can never rise up and open the gates of heaven. "Without Me," said Jesus Christ, "*ye* can do nothing. *I* am the Way, the Truth, and the Life."

I wish to lay a stress upon this, because I fear that many of us are apt to forget that "every good and perfect gift cometh from above." We know how very easy it is for men to plume themselves, in worldly matters, on qualities which are not of their own production. Does not he who boasts of his noble race, and walks as if he felt the blood of generations of princes circulating through his veins, often forget that he was not the founder of his line? Are not those who have beauty of countenance, or grace of figure, often oblivious that these are gifts, in originating which they had no part? Does not the strong man glory, as if he himself had given the iron force to his muscles? and the clever man assume airs, as if he had fashioned the fine texture of his subtle brain? Surely, we see these things every day. Yes; and there is such a disease as self-righteous vanity in things of the Spirit. It is possible to do a good action, and afterwards forget that our power came from the Holy Ghost! It is possible to conquer an evil habit, and to sound our Pharisaic trumpets, as if we had made the weapons of victory ourselves! It is possible to rise from the dreadful death of sin, and after we have been, for a time, clear of the rottenness of the tomb, and have had our grave-clothes unloosed, to forget Who it was that said, "Lazarus, come forth"! There are many revolting kinds of ungratefulness in the world, but there is none that we should dread so much as that self-righteous vanity which forgets Jesus Christ, and tries to walk in its own strength, after being quickened and supported by Him. Alas for that soul which has grown cold towards "the Sower," and has lost the sweet savour of His name! Alas for the Christian who, having been arrayed in the bridal-garment of grace by the very King

Himself, shall dream, even for an hour, that *he* by his own skill wove the unearthly robe lustrous with the jewels of the Spirit!

"Behold, the Sower *went forth.*" The first ideas suggested to the mind by this expression are the following. "To go forth," signifies that the sower leaves his usual home for another spot; there is a point of departure and a point of arrival. Next, the ground does not move towards the sower, but the sower moves towards the ground. Moreover, the sower and the soil, although closely united in one work, are yet distinct. These general thoughts will clear the way for your understanding the deep meaning which lies beneath the words "going forth." What, then, is the mystery, what is the great truth, hidden in the folds of these words of the parable? The Sower is the Second Person of the ever-blessed Trinity; God the Wisdom of the Father; God of God; Light of Light; Very God of Very God. The Sower was from eternity in the bosom of the Father; He was God, and is God, and shall be God, for ever and ever. There came, however, an hour when, out of His unspeakable love to us, the Father "sent forth His Son." "By this," writes St. John, "hath the charity of God appeared towards us; because God hath sent His only-begotten Son into the world" (1 John iv. 9). The will of the Father being the same as the will of the Son, the words "sending forth" on the part of the Father are substantially just the same as the "going forth" on the part of the Son. He "went forth:" this indicates the perfect freedom of the act; freely the Father sent the Son, and freely the Son obeyed. Behold, the Sower went forth. Mystery of mysteries! From the eternity of the Godhead the Son of God went forth into time; from the bosom of the unbegotten Father the Son went into the womb of the creature: the Infinite clothed Himself with the finite. The first soil that this divine Sower approached was the flesh and soul of His human nature; to this the Godhead went forth, being distinct from, yet joined to it by a marvellous union; for the Word became flesh, and the Son of God went forth, in order that He might for our salvation become the Son of Mary. The first moment, therefore, of His conception by Mary was the beginning of this amazing journey of God. What an idea, moreover, do we obtain of the greatness of the Blessed Virgin, when we remember that this conception did not take place until Mary said to the Angel, "Be it unto me according to thy word"! It is a truth wonderful beyond all thought, that the Second Person of the Holy Trinity, He whose love for us had been burning bright for ages before our creation—He our God—He our Saviour, was waiting in the abyss of the Trinity—waiting for the creation of Mary—waiting for her free consent—waiting for the fiat of His own creature, and not stirring until she, by inspiration, pronounced the words, "Be it unto me according to thy word." And then, as a giant longing to run his course, the Son of God sped into the womb of Mary from the bosom of the Father; then, the great Sower of salvation "went forth," then, and not until then. Who can fathom the humility of such an act? for this "going forth" was not from low to high;

it was the reverse. When a prisoner leaves his prison for a palace—when a slave becomes free—when a poverty-stricken man exchanges his rags and scanty fare for wealth and comfort—when the servant becomes a master—when the dying man revives—when the warrior goes to receive his chaplet of victory,—all these are "goings forth" which are full of joy. Who would not choose them? Far different was that of the "Sower." He was God, and He went forth to become a man; He was free, and He went to be the servant of sinners; He was full of glory, and He emptied Himself of it; being rich, for our sakes He became poor; millions and millions of Angels were ever prostrate before Him, and yet He submitted to the scorn of men. Yes, as far as He could do such an act, God became an outcast. He banished Himself from His own Paradise to come into this vale of tears. The Second Adam became a kind of first Adam; He trod the earth in sorrow, fulfilling, in a mystical sense, and working out its primeval curse— "Thorns and thistles shall it bring forth to thee" (Gen. iii. 18); and wetting it with His own blood, in gory sweat in the garden of Gethsemane, and in torrents upon the cross. Was there ever such a Sower known as the Son of Man? For the very nature which He had taken and glorified and had sown with His Godhead, rose up against Him in the persons of others, and those of His own household wounded the very hands that blessed them.

Let me ask you if you consider, as you ought, the astonishing love and patience that there must have been in the Son of God, to have induced Him to undergo such a work. Do we not all become in some degree hardened by familiarity with well-known truths? Just as in nature we are so accustomed to the regularity of the seasons, to the shining of the sun and falling of rain, that we fancy it is a kind of mechanism that must go on by itself; forgetting that even these things are signs of the perpetually present love of God; so we act, alas, amidst the marvels of grace. The words of the Creed in which we profess our belief that God became man lose, by habit, their flavour. We know that eighteen hundred years ago the "Sower went forth" to humiliation; but do we estimate as we ought the motive which drew Him forth? Do we remember, as we should, that He went forth for our sakes, and not for His own? Ordinary sowers require to sow, in order to obtain the necessary food for their life. But the Son of God had no such need. What could He want Who was Life itself? What joy could He want Who was Bliss Eternal? What glory could He desire Who was God? It was love and pity that drew Him forth, as with mighty cords, from the enrapturing solitude of His Godhead into this world of sin. He saw how barren, how parched, how thirsty, how thorn-beset were the nature and life of fallen man; and so He went forth to raise him up, to heal, to fertilise, and quicken him for glory. "For this is charity; not as though *we* had loved God, but because He *hath first loved* us." Observe also the perseverance and singleness of purpose in the Sower. He went forth to sow. Full well the Son of God knew that His work would be often hindered—full well He knew that much of the seed He spread would return no fruit. He saw beforehand the power of the devil, and the ungratefulness and iniquity of men. He knew that His incarnation would be to many a dreadful judgment instead of salvation. Nevertheless, His patience and perseverance were equal to His love. One great thought was before Him, one great work, one great sacrifice. "I have a baptism," He said, "wherewith to be baptised; and how am I straitened until it be accomplished!" Jesus Christ came not for His own pleasure, or honour, or reward. He came to "seek and to save that which was lost." Behold, the Sower went forth *to sow*. Men and bad angels may oppose Him; the sky may lower and the lightning flash, and the very earth reel with commotion, and the powers of this world may do their worst, but *nothing can stop the sowing of Jesus Christ*. He will do His work upon the soil, whether there be a return or not. Is not this a solemn reflection for all of us? Let us often examine our hearts and see whether we are alive to the fact, that no less a sower than God is dealing with our souls, and dealing with them perpetually. It is He who pricks our consciences with salutary remorse; it is He who chastises us with necessary afflictions; it is He who inspires us with encouragement, and draws our reluctant wills gently on to more self-sacrificing efforts to do His will.

The Church infallibly teaches us divine doctrine, and the Sacraments minister sanctification, and good Angels guide and defend us from evil, and the blessed Saints pray for us. But we must never forget or undervalue another truth, namely, that all these things are secondary to the Sower Himself; they are but His channels of communication — His servants. Behind and above the visible body of the Church; behind all Popes, Bishops, and Priests; behind the seven Sacraments; from the beginning of Christianity, and at the present moment, in all lands and at all times, stands the Sower Himself, the Incarnate Word. The years, days, and hours pass on, and generations come and go; but He the Unchangeable, the Faithful One, never forsakes the work of His love. With Him this life, however wasted by others, and transitory, is always a seed-time. At first He sowed the earth visibly, for He was upon it; men heard His words, and saw His actions. After His Ascension He sowed, and still sows His seed invisibly, yet not the less certainly or powerfully.

But the hour is fast approaching when He will come again; not to sow, but to reap with the awful sickle of judgment, and the purifying fan in His hand, which shall separate eternally the wheat from the chaff. Are you reflecting seriously upon this second coming of the Sower? Are you preparing for that in which you believe? As He went forth at the appointed hour to sow the world with "grace and truth," so in like manner, and with the same inflexible exactness—the punctuality of God—He will come to judge the living and the dead. At a moment unexpected the trumpet of the Archangel will sound, and the clouds will part asunder, and the everlasting gates will lift up their heads once more, and Jesus the

King of Glory will issue forth to punish the wicked with eternal death, and to reward the good with eternal life. "Wherefore be you also ready; because at what hour ye know not, the Son of Man will come" (Matt. xxiv. 44).

"I saw, and behold, a white cloud, and upon the cloud one sitting like to the Son of Man, having on His head a crown of gold, and *in His hand a sharp sickle*. And another Angel came out from the Temple, crying with a loud voice to Him that sat upon the cloud, Thrust in Thy sickle, and reap; because the hour is come to reap, for the harvest of the earth is ripe. And He that sat upon the cloud thrust His sickle into the earth, and the earth was reaped" (Apoc. xiv. 14-16).

II.

PROFESSION WITHOUT EARNESTNESS.

"Whilst he soweth, some fell by the wayside, and the birds of the air came and ate them up." *Matthew* xiii. 4.

It has been explained that the Sower in the parable is no less a person than Jesus Christ, the Son of God and the Son of Man. We have now to ascertain what the seed was which He "went forth" in order to sow. The word "seed," if interpreted in its widest sense, embraces in its signification everything which our Lord was and is—everything which He said and did for the world into which He came. He Himself, the God-Man, is both the Sower and the Seed.

His nature is Seed, for through It our nature is enabled to grow up into a holy and glorified humanity; through the oneness of that Seed we are enabled to leave our state of separation from God, and to be joined with Him. Thus, as St. Peter writes, we are "made partakers of the Divine Nature." The gifts of grace that flow down upon us so abundantly from Him, have the power to quicken our hearts if we will allow them; the example that He set; the virtues which we call preëminently Christian—such as humility, singleness of purpose, purity, and love of God and man; above all, the sufferings which He chose to endure for our sake, from His conception in Mary's womb to His death upon Calvary,—all these are the *seed-grains* of the Sower. Whether they were dropped in Bethlehem, or Nazareth, or Jerusalem; whether in the midst of multitudes, or in the solitude of the lonely mountain; whether when He was accompanied by Peter and James and John, or led by the Spirit into the Wilderness, and by Satan carried alone to the pinnacle of the Temple; when He was fasting forty days and nights, or sanctifying innocent and social festivity at Cana—however varied the circumstances might be—the Sower and the Seed were ever the same. Taken in its fullest sense, the Seed is coextensive with the Person of Jesus Christ; it includes His nature and His work, with all His gifts to, and operations upon, the souls of men.

There is, however, a more limited sense of the "seed." When our Lord comes to explain His parable, He evidently means by the seed which is sown to speak of the *doctrines* which He taught. The seed, therefore, in the parable signifies the whole Gospel of Jesus Christ, —the words He uttered; the truths He commanded to be believed in by every one, Jew and Gentile; and the duties which He commanded to be done. There is the law of divine revelation, which is intended to inform and guide our minds, in other words, the Christian creed; and there is also the law of conduct, the Christian commandments, which teach us our duty to God and our neighbour. These taken together are the seed particularly mentioned in the parable; and His meaning is fully expressed by our Lord in one phrase, "*the word of the kingdom.*" It is the message of our Redeemer to us. Observe, also, that it includes not only such great facts as that of the Incarnation, Resurrection, and future Judgment, but it extends to all the teachings of Christ and His Apostles about the Church and Sacraments. For the seed, to use our Divine Lord's expression, is the word *of the kingdom;* not of the King only, but also of His spiritual empire upon earth: it therefore includes all that He taught about the powers and rights of His Church. Everything which is true about the Church of Christ, its commandments, and claims, and instructions—all these are contained in "the word of the kingdom." It is deserving of remark, too, that by His very language our Lord teaches us the inseparable unity of His Gospel. He does not say the *words,* but the *word* of the kingdom. The real gospel is not a series of fragments, still less of discords: it is *one* seed, *one* law. This idea is also conveyed by the expression "the kingdom." For Christ does not speak of the word of the *kingdoms,* as if there were many independent churches, yet all possessing one and the same creed. The kingdom is one, and its word is one. As the Sower is one, so also is the seed.

We now come to consider the ground upon which the seed fell; and here, at once, we are struck with a very impressive fact. The seed is ever the same: that is to say, the Gospel-truth never alters; time rolls on, but the seed never moulders or turns to corruption. No wickedness of man, no craft of the devil, has any power to destroy or lessen the fertilising properties of the doctrine of Christ. Far different is it with the ground: *that* can change, and does change. The souls of men can be fit for the seed of the Word of God, and by the tremendous power of self-will can be altered so as to become unfit. When a soul corresponds with the teaching of Jesus Christ,—when it receives and thoroughly takes it into its being,—then there is harmony between the seed and the soil. But when the soul of any man, through some fault of its own, does not receive the Gospel thoroughly into its understanding and affections, then the seed of the Sower is dropped in vain; then there is division between the seed and the ground; then the powers of "the word of the kingdom," wonderful and life-giving as they are in themselves, are rendered useless. This is a solemn fact of itself: it is a solemn fact that you and I can, by the exercise of our free-will, stop our sanctification, and put a bar to the intention of God. The Gospel may shine brightly before us, and we can put a screen up before the eyes of our soul, so that the rays shall be shut out, or come in with only a faint and sickly glimmer. This is of itself enough to make us serious; still more grave is another fact that we learn from the parable. Our Lord mentions four different kinds of ground, on which the divine seed falls: that is, He describes four different states of the soul; and out of the four, how many, think you, receive the teaching of God to their salvation? Only *one*—one out of four. The three others are fatal to any good or lasting effect of the Sower's seed. Three out of four kinds of souls that are enumerated, misuse the gift of salvation. The first state of soul is described by the following figure of speech: "The sower went forth to sow, and whilst he soweth, some fell by the wayside." In England we are accustomed to think of sowing-ground as a field kept quite separate from the high-road; and we can hardly at first understand how the seed sown by the husbandman could possibly manage to fall into the common path. In many other countries, and in the East particularly, very often, no such care is taken to fence-in the land; so that the soil might easily run to the edges of the public road, and hardly be divided from it. In such a case the ground would be unfit for seed; for, besides being hard and dusty, it would be exposed to accidents. It would seem no man's property, and the seed would be tossed to and fro by the feet of passers-by.

Now, what classes of persons are fairly represented by the "wayside"? The first contains those who know the Christian religion well, and do not value it. The "word of the kingdom" is in their possession; they are Catholics, who are so far from being ignorant of the true Faith, that perhaps they frequently boast of professing "the old religion." From their infancy a good and tender mother has taught their young lips to pray; the Catechism is to them as a familiar tale—they know it by heart. They know how to confess, and how to prepare for the Holy Communion; the precepts of the Church are clearly and deeply engraved on their memories. In short, they have the right seed, the divine Gospel. But there is one terrible fault which will be their ruin. They do not cherish and love their religion. Their creed is written on their brain, and it never goes deeper. Their Christianity is an accurate photograph on their memories; but like other photographs it is not the *reality*—there is no life and movement in their interior. The truth has come from the glorious sun of the gospel of the kingdom; but it is only an image pictured on the thin tissue of their minds. They do not value this knowledge above all other science. As they know history or geography or mechanics, so they know their religion. "Ye *know* these things," said our Lord; "*happy are ye if ye do them.*" Is it not a fact that there are many Catholics who cannot pretend to any ignorance of their duties, and yet who neglect habitually the most urgent duties? What is the use of their knowledge, if they never carry it out? What is the use of their faith, if they have no love? What is the use of their being able to talk about the holy Sacraments, if they are strangers to the Confessional, and are unknown at the altar of the Bread of Life? They are not on the highroad of a false creed—be it so; but if their hearts are untouched by the faith they believe in, it is much the same in the end: a seed that is on the wayside has no more chance of bringing forth fruit to eternal life than the broad, high-road itself, upon whose hard surface no seed whatever is found.

A second class represented by the "wayside" consists of those who are too idle or indifferent to guard their souls from evil. If you desire to have a certain and abundant harvest, you must keep your soil to itself; you must fence it clearly off from the common path, and the fences must be often examined; and where found to be faulty, they must be renewed and strengthened. Now all this demands labour and vigilance; fences will not make themselves, gaps will not fill up by magic, nor will they even be perceived to exist at all, unless a pair of vigilant eyes takes the trouble to look at their condition.

The "wayside" is a figure, then, of the slothful Christian. O, the thousands of good-meaning, easy-going Christians who never advance a step in religion; nay, who are perpetually falling back, because they will not take the pains to protect themselves from evil. The seed must have the soil to itself; and so it is with our hearts; there is a constant tendency in all of us to fall away into the common road of indulgence; and there is no safety unless we take pains to put a yoke on our desires. How many there are who say that they wish to be good! they long to be meek, and pure, and spiritual; and yet, if their life is examined, it is discovered that they *do nothing* to effectuate these wishes. We must make rules about prayer, and keep to them; we must make rules about the way in which we ought to spend our time or money. We must put fixed limits on our eating, drinking, and sleeping. We must determine to avoid the society of persons dangerous to our innocence, and places which, if frequented, are almost sure to unfit us for devotion. We must secure some quiet for our spirits, in order that our good thoughts may have time to ripen. We must give a certain time to spiritual reading. These are fences absolutely necessary for the soul. What, then, is the reason of our neglect? What is the reason that with all our fine resolutions, and wishes, and talking, and sentimentality, we remain hard and unfruitful ground, and cannot be distinguished from the common run of men, who make no claim to any kind of piety? What is the reason? What else but our sloth; what but our love of ease and quiet, and our hatred of being under any system of rules? Let none be deceived; the Gospel of Christ, the Catholic faith, cannot bring forth fruit, if we leave our hearts unfenced from temptation to sin.

The "wayside" is also a figure of those who, though, as Christians, they profess to belong to the religion of the Cross, yet are thorough lovers of the world. They do not commit any great crime; they do not outrage the proprieties of Christianity by conspicuous, open scandals. But their main object is to live for the present; from morning to night their thought is of the world; they love its ways and its fashions, and are insensibly governed by its unspiritual principles. St. John says, "Love *not* the world. He that loveth the world, the love of the Father is *not* in him;" but these Christians hear not the voice. Just as a man standing at the side of a crowded thoroughfare is absorbed by what he hears and sees, so it is with this class of Christians. The great world rolls past them with its vain noise, its slanderous detractions, its silly chatter about nothing, and its pomp and show and fashionable vices; and these Christians enjoy it, and love it, and almost wish they could plunge more entirely into the fascinating whirl. They follow the world as the way*side* runs parallel with the "way" itself, being a part of it, covered with its dust, and sharing in the scenes which occur upon it.

The Gospel of Jesus Christ has no chance in thoroughly worldly hearts. How can they think upon such words as these: "Take up thy cross *daily*, and follow Me," when they are doing their very best to escape all crosses? How can they dwell seriously on such truths as this: "It is appointed unto all men once to die, and then the judgment;" or, "What does it profit a man if he gain the whole world and suffer the loss of his own soul?" when the present hour and present enjoyment are to them a passion? How can they expect to pray well, and be recollected, when the people they mix with and love most are doing all they can to banish sacred thoughts and conversation, for fear of spoiling their worldly happiness? No, my brethren, let us be convinced that we cannot be on the side of the world and in the field of the Lord at the same time. We may have the "word of the kingdom" in our faith; but if we live the life of worldlings, the seed will remain barren; it will be trampled about in the dust, and will produce only a heavy judgment at the day of account.

"Whilst he soweth, some fell by the wayside, and the birds of the air came and ate them up." These "birds of the air" are of various kinds; their name is legion. The foremost amongst them, the most malignant, the most unwearied, and the most disguised,—the natural enemy of the seed, the bird that if driven away returns again with a frightful audacity, the bird that is ever learning fresh modes of approach, and never forgets past experience, is the one indicated, especially, by our Lord Himself in His explanation of this parable. "When anyone heareth the word of the kingdom, and understandeth it not, then cometh *the wicked one*, and catcheth away that which was sown in his heart." This is Satan, the "Prince of the Powers of the Air." To this robber, an idle, unguarded, wayside-soul is an easy prey. Such a soul is a temptation to the devil himself; it gives, if I may say so, the bird-call, inviting the devil up, if he be

not already present, from the bottomless pit.
Looking like a small insignificant bird, he is
full of evil strength and dreadful tenacity. How
subtle he is in his approaches; how noiseless!
How he seems to have gone away entirely, when,
as at the temptation of Christ, it is only for
a while; he is merely wheeling round, or dis-
appearing into a cloud for concealment, until
he can return. He makes, occasionally, direct
and visible attacks, as is testified in the lives
of St. Antony and other Saints. The object,
however, of such assaults as these is to weary,
annoy, and mock, rather than to seduce. His
ordinary plan is described by the word "catcheth away;" he is a stealthy, rapid thief, pur-
loining what is good in us, by degrees; using
instruments that are often in themselves innocent, but under certain circumstances dangerous. He robs us through different pretexts;
as when he persuades us to take unnecessary
rest, under a false plea of weakness or weariness.
He robs us by suggesting occupations that will
draw us off from our plain duty. He robs us by
throwing in our way acquaintances whose inti-

macy will in the end lower our notions of right. He cannot, however, succeed in carrying away the seed completely, unless we belong to the class described by our Lord as those who do not understand the word of the kingdom. "When one heareth the word of the kingdom, and *understandeth it not*, there cometh the wicked one, and catcheth away that which was sown in the heart." If the seed has obtained no firm entrance in the heart; if it lies upon it rather than in it; if the "kingdom" be not embraced by the will; if it be not a practical subject of frequent meditation; if it stamps no mark upon our daily life; if we are not changed by the sowing of the seed, and have not its germinating qualities inwrought into our principles,—then the "word of the kingdom" has not been understood according to the sense meant by our Lord. If we *do* understand, then, although the evil one may try to pounce upon the seed, and although we may tremble lest he should lift it up, still his efforts will be in vain; for Jesus Christ the Sower will guard the seed which He has planted in a faithful heart, and no one shall "pluck it out of His hand." The vigilant and laborious Christian need not be afraid. "Be pleased, O Lord, to deliver me; look down, O Lord, to help me: let them be confounded and ashamed together that seek after my soul to take it away" (Ps. xxxix. 14, 15).

"Resist the devil, and *he will fly from you*" (James iv. 7). Besides the Prince of the Powers of the Air there are other birds which do us enormous mischief. Among them, without dilating at large upon them, may be mentioned useless occupations. There is an activity which is real work, and there is an activity which is only another form of idleness. "Who," said a Saint of old, "shall restore me that day spent in trifling?" *That* day; only one day that he could remember! How many days have we frittered away in trifles! How we have allowed paltry attentions to paltry things to catch away that seed of precious time that no bird of the air will ever bring back! Let us think of our uncalled-for meddlings, and fussy coöperations with persons as idle as ourselves; let us think of the stupid, aimless conversations that we have indulged in by the hour; let us think of our self-made distractions, our excessive diversions and pastimes, our profitless acts too of curiosity: were not all these so many pilferings of precious seed?

Venial sins are birds of the air also; very small in size, yet most noxious to the soul. True, a venial sin does not carry off all grace; yet the habit of caring little about these sins will, in the end, lead to the worst of consequences. Though one small bird cannot do much to destroy a large quantity of seed, nevertheless a number of small birds following each other rapidly will do great injury. So it is with venial sins; if they are deliberately committed, and if there is no anxiety to avoid them for the future, their number will grow with an astonishing increase. Sooner also than we have any idea they will blunt the conscience, weaken good habits, and prepare the way for sins of a deeper dye. Speaking of venial sins, St. Leonard of Port Maurice exclaims in his Spiritual Exercises, "Either the Saints were wrong, or we are wrong. They lived with the greatest caution; we live with the greatest liberty. The Saints thought much of every small hindrance in the direct way of eternal salvation; we walk without a bridle along the ruinous paths of eternal perdition. The Saints endeavoured to avoid the slightest defect in order to be free from even an apparent danger; we, with extreme audacity despising little falls, disport ourselves on the edge of the precipice." Again, "O what a splendid sum of merits do these household pilferers steal from us under our very eyes!" St. Catherine of Genoa had one venial sin represented to her interiorly in a vision; and so appalling was the sight, that she declared that if she had not been divinely supported, her body would have gone to pieces from horror and loathing. Upon this St. Leonard remarks, "If the mere shadow of one venial sin renders the soul so deformed, reflect what a loathsome aspect must your soul present, which is not guilty of one venial sin only, but of numbers upon numbers, and these, too, considerable in quantity, in quality, in malice and pertinacity." No man will watch vigilantly against these "birds of the air," unless he has learned first to recognise them under every disguise, and to fear their consequences. How can this be, unless we cultivate delicacy of conscience, aim steadily at higher perfection than we have attained, and flee unnecessary temptations? "He that contemneth small things shall fall little by little," says Solomon (Ecclus. xix. 1); and "he that loveth danger shall perish in it" (ibid. iii. 27).

There is another class of birds which are exceedingly dangerous. They can fly with amazing rapidity; and springing up, as they do, out of our own minds, they are not readily detected. Often, too, like birds of beautiful plumage and melodious in their fascinating song, they succeed in robbing us almost before we are aware of what is passing. How many woes come to us! How much delicacy of conscience, how many heaven-born aspirations to a higher degree of perfection, how many consolations that we should have otherwise enjoyed, are caught up from us by these invisible, silent, yet dangerous creatures! I refer to evil thoughts of every kind. Who that is wise does not fear them? Who is free from this temptation? The subject, however, is so important, and frequently so much neglected by many of us, that it deserves a discourse to itself.

III.

EVIL THOUGHTS.

"The birds of the air came and ate them up." *Matt.* xiii. 4.

WHEN we speak of a man's life that is past, or when we try and consider our own life as yet unfinished, we usually picture to our minds a mass of actions that have been done, pleasures enjoyed, or sufferings that have been endured. There is a vast portion of life that can never be chronicled. Who can pretend to tell all that he has done, good or evil, useful or unprofitable, during a single year? Still more impossible is it to remember and record what has formed itself into language since the first hour when we became answerable for our words. Who amongst us can think of the conversations we have begun deliberately ourselves, and the answers we have given to others, the hints and allusions that have escaped, as we say, from our lips, with scarcely any reflection,

—words of sudden passion, words of vanity,—sparks flying off the tongue under momentary excitement? Unquestionably, the words of few men are recorded and handed down to posterity; and yet the words of every man, considered as a responsible creature of God, form a very large item in life.

If this remark be true in regard to words, then still more is it true with regard to thoughts. There are many limits to other parts of our life: we cannot always be speaking—we cannot always be doing even our ordinary outward actions; for occasions fail us, and fatigue tells us to stop even when we are inclined to go on. With thoughts, however, it is different; as long as we are awake we *must* think; the brain vibrates with the pulsation of ideas as regularly as, and far more quickly than, the heart beats with the pulsation of its currents of blood. Ideas more or less formed, impressions more or less vivid of present objects, wishes and intentions about the future, and images of past thoughts, are constantly streaming up from the soul in an astounding abundance, so rapid that we cannot measure their speed, so subtle that we cannot grasp and analyse their exact nature, so numerous that we cannot count them with any approach to certainty of accuracy. If our thoughts for even a month were all to be placed before us in some way that would be plain to our outward senses; if we could hear each of them sounding with some intelligible voice, or see them tinted with some distinct colour, or massed together in one collected bulk, there is not one among us who would not be utterly amazed and perhaps awe-struck at their variety and quantity. We are indeed, all of us—the most ignorant as well as the most learned—teeming with sensations and conscious yearnings every hour; thought of some kind or other is as the very breathing of our mysterious rational nature. For much of this brain-activity of ours, we are not at all responsible. We have sometimes no more power over our thoughts than we have over the involuntary jerking of a muscle. We can no more prevent them than we can stop ourselves from being in a glow during heat, or from shivering during cold. On the other hand, there is a vast quantity for which we *are* most strictly answerable; there are countless thoughts of ours which will be as truly called before the bar of judgment, and as certainly weighed in the balance of God's holiness, as any actions, plain to the eye of man, that we ever committed with the members of our body. There is indeed one difference which is in favour of the deeds of the body, and it is this: whereas no act of the body—no act, for instance, of the eye, or the tongue, or the touch—can have any guilt in the sight of God unless it be accompanied by the inward will, yet there is a fearful quantity of sin that can be committed by the soul, without the body taking any visible part in it whatever. There are many causes which have a tendency to make us forget, or at least undervalue, the real sinfulness of wrong thoughts.

Of the numerous reasons why the mass of Christians underrate the guilt of this particular sin, I will mention the following. In the first place, this error springs from a narrow, low estimate of sin in general. Men for the most part think lightly of any sin which does not palpably affect their fellow-men. They can understand that there is guilt in falsehood, guilt in robbery, guilt in calumny, guilt in violence, guilt in corrupting the morals of others. Sin, broadly considered, is in their estimation something done by them which directly injures their fellow-creatures. So strongly ingrained is this idea in the minds even of many Catholics, who have been taught better, that they hold themselves comparatively innocent if they can say that they are clear of robbery, injustice, and the like. They may have almost forgotten God; they may have neglected to pray to Him, and may have used His holy Name most irreverently. But those sins do not press upon their conscience. They do not stand definitely out before their soul as grave iniquities; it requires argument to make them feel that they are, through them, in great danger of losing their salvation. What is the cause of this singular dulness and blindness? It is a want of clearly discerning that sin is *anything* deliberately done by the will of man against the will of God. It is the tendency of all of us, living as we do in a world of fellow-men, and feeling our interests closely bound up with theirs, to look at sin as though it were chiefly some open outrage upon *their rights or comforts*. The result is, that whilst man's rights are magnified, the offences which affect the rights of God more directly, look small and are little regarded. The soul forgets that it is bound to obey God in all things, and therefore in every desire and imagination; and the end is, that man sins freely and easily if the offence be one which is against God alone, or does not manifestly interfere with those around us.

The guilt of evil thoughts is underrated also because of their secrecy. Public opinion, as it is called, has a vast influence upon private opinion : if a number of tongues are ready to proclaim our fault, if a number of keen eyes are watching us, if what we are going to do is likely to be marked by a thousand ready fingers as a blot upon our character, it is astonishing how quickly we ourselves learn to have the same opinion of our own action. We look through the public conscience, as through an infallible glass, into our own deeds; and by a sort of instinct, we echo back loudly the condemnation which, if we had been left to ourselves, would perhaps have been very slight indeed. Does not a child learn a great deal of the real nature of its faults from the severe look and tone of the mother? and are we not all accustomed to judge of our faults by the estimate of our friends and associates? Observe, then, how this fact of daily experience tells upon our judgment of sins of thought. Here all is secret; we are sure that there is no circle of watchers around us with eyes keen enough to peer into the cabinet of the brain; the soul moves more boldly along in its evil path, because it is aware that no human steps are dogging its course; it is robbing God by some unworthy thought, some thought of revenge, or vanity, or envy, or lust; but the tread is stealthy, the weapon is covered; the soul strikes at the pure law of God, yet not a sound betrays the fact of the unnatural blow. The effect of all which privacy is, that we ourselves begin to imagine the sin to be far less than it is in reality. It seems light to us, although in truth it is, as Solomon says, "an abomination to the Lord" (Prov. xv. 26). It seems light, because we judge of it by our own conscience alone; that conscience being more or less bribed by our evil desires. Spectators are not with us; the evil thought is part of a wicked drama which the heart is performing in private: there is no barometer to show how low the soul is sinking. Alas, God is before us, and around us, and within us; that God Whose thoughts are not as our thoughts, and Who is a discerner of the heart to its inmost core; but unless we are in the habit of referring all things to Him, whether secret or open, the idea of His presence will be as dim to us as that of His holiness.

Another reason for our undervaluing this particular kind of sin is the absence of its traces afterwards. There are many sins that print unmistakable marks of themselves upon this outer world; we cannot well forget them if we would. Like the blood-stained hands of a murderer, they leave tell-tale signs behind them, which are ever crying out, Guilt, Guilt!

A calumniator has withered some fair reputation, and the ruin of that good name stares him grimly in the face: perhaps the calumny has brought with it loss of employment, and starvation to a wife and children, and the beggared man rises up constantly like a spectre before the heartless maligner; for they live in the same world and are perpetually crossing each other's path. Many a son, by his disobedience and dissipation, has broken a mother's heart, and her grave can never be seen by him without recalling the bitterness of a past which is beyond all remedy. A father who is a drunkard lives to watch with horror the rank wickedness of those children whose lips he has taught to thirst for the poison which has ruined himself, and to curse savagely the very parent who has brought them into the world. Numerous are the iniquities which, having been carried out into full accomplishment, proclaim daily and hourly to the sinner himself the grievousness of his offence. Often the sight of the wreck and misery thus produced ends in his repentance. "What shall I do," he cries out, "to be saved?" Not so is it with sins of thought; they are crimes that do not cry aloud; the ruin they make is within, rather than without, and the devastation of the soul is as secret as the sin; it is a fire that burns and withers without any visible blaze or smoke. And, as it leaves no manifest token outside, so it is rapidly forgotten. For the moment, an evil thought, willingly indulged in, may prick the conscience and sadden the spirit; but how soon it is forgotten! other thoughts come in to whirl it away in their greater current; and though it once left a pang behind, now both the thought and the pang have passed away like shadows, leaving not a vestige behind. They are all written in God's book of judgment; there they stand clearly and awfully distinct; but the memory of them in the sinner's soul is as blank as if no stain had ever defiled its pages. Is it not, then, terribly easy to think too lightly of sins which, besides being secret and noiseless, are followed by so few manifest effects in the world, and fade away so quickly from the accusing tablet of the conscience?

Evil Thoughts.

When we speak of evil thoughts as being sins, we must understand the word "evil" in its strict sense. We mean such movements of the mind, such desires, such imaginations, as are under our control. Thoughts about evil are not necessarily evil thoughts. The mind is so constituted, and the power of association so great, that ideas frequently enter it and challenge our attention, without any coöperation on our side. Sometimes bad thoughts will start up on a sudden, and stand before us fully formed; no one can tell how or why they appear: we have not encouraged or called them; yet there they are, as though they had been noiselessly painted on the soul (which doubtless is often the case) by some unseen malicious spirit. Sometimes a holy thought will be followed by an unrighteous one so quickly, and apparently so naturally, that they seem parts of one idea; as if they were the light and shade of the same object. At other times, by some mysterious mental mechanism, a whole mass of dangerous ideas will revolve before us, turning as it were upon the pin-point of some one little phantasy, which we had carelessly allowed to enter the mind. We considered it was a trifle, and so in itself it was: we deemed it to be alone, when it was the advanced guard of a whole army of iniquitous imaginations, which follow each in close procession through the mind. Then again, there are a thousand things in the world which we cannot escape, and yet which bring evil of some kind or other before our consciousness. We hear bad words in the streets; we read histories in which deeds of wickedness are recorded; and we study for scientific purposes much that is dangerous to purity of heart. Then there are countless things which suggest evil because they are practically temptations; things in themselves harmless, yet which to our fallen nature bring the thought of wrong, even though we may wish it away, and succeed in resisting the temptation. Nay, how can we even watch against any specific sin, how can we detest it, how can we devise means to battle with it, without in some fashion or other having sin present to the understanding? It is clear that these are not the kinds of evil thoughts for which we shall be condemned. These are "birds of the air," which fly near to, but do not *eat up*, the good seed. That which constitutes guilt is something for which we ourselves are answerable; something which we know at the moment is wrong, or, at all events, likely to lead us into evil; something which we can, by grace and effort, prevent our will from welcoming and embracing. And here it may be useful to remind you that an evil thought may be most vividly present to the fancy, without any fault on our part at all. The imagination and the will are very distinct faculties; evil may haunt our imagination in every shape; it may cleave to our mind as though it were a part of its substance: it may remain there, just as if some one, unrolling before us a voluptuous picture, and illuminating every part with a powerful light, were to hold our eyes open, and force them to look at the repulsive details. Yet, during all this time, we may be guilty of no sin whatever; for if our will stands on guard, and, like the Angel in Paradise waving its sword, keeps the evil thought from entering our inner heart, then no guilt is contracted. The wicked idea remains there and will not vanish; but its breath does not harm us; we have no fellowship with it; it is an odious apparition in the chambers of the understanding, and nothing more: we may be sufferers, for we cannot at the moment dissolve it into air; but we are not sinners. Our inward protest, our detestation, and fear are our victory.

Nevertheless, whilst we make every proper and just distinction, and whilst we admit fully that we must not confound temptation with sin, and vividness of imagination with real consent, there still remains the fact that genuine sins of thought *are* committed by Christians with a frequency and intensity of guilt of which God alone knows the full measure. They are committed by the young in the first gambols of their ever-active fancy; in whom also curiosity has the force of a passion, inciting them to indulge in thoughts about sins which as yet, perhaps, they have not dared to carry out into action. They are committed by the old, in whom a guilty course during their earlier years has planted the sad habit of a polluted imagination, which seems to taint with unhallowed associations everything that passes through its gates. There is no class, no sex, no age free from the danger; there is no place where evil thoughts will not try to intrude: before the holy Tabernacle, and in the very act of Communion, it is possible for them to be entertained. We know too well that souls have perished when within an inch of eternity. Men in the face of imminent death, with a distinct knowledge that in another hour they must stand naked before their God, thus hanging by a hair over the great abyss, have deliberately consented to an evil thought, and been therefore carried away into instant damnation.

There are many remedies against this special sin; the chief being, according to all spiritual writers, prayer and mortification of the senses, for through the senses mainly come our dangerous thoughts; but there are three in particular, without which the others will be of little avail. The first is, that you must learn to fear and detest sin *of any kind*, as being an offence against God. Do not measure sin by its grossness only, or by its effects upon others, or by its supposed influence upon your own soul; learn to abhor it as a personal outrage against God Himself—as a cruelty and indignity to Jesus Christ. By this means, you will learn to look at a sin of thought, although known only to God and yourself, as an offence equally real with, and often worse in malignity than, many other sins that are more outward and conspicuous. It is not the deadliest weapon that always makes the most noise.

Be careful especially in watching the first movements of your mind in the direction of danger. A great part of the guilt incurred by our thoughts is owing to this neglect. Men, through carelessness or laxity of conscience, allow their imagination to wander at will, without control, until at last they find themselves first tasting, and then feeding habitually on, that which is poison to the soul.

Lastly, let it be a constant study to fill

the mind with holy, or at least innocent, reflections. The mind never can be entirely empty: if not preoccupied with good, then evil will flow in by a kind of natural gravitation. If God is not upon His throne in the centre of the soul, then the Wicked One will glide in, and, in one shape or other, will virtually occupy the place. If you take pains to have the thought of God's presence, of His love, and beauty, and glory; if you practise acts of fellowship with the Angels and Saints by prayer, aspirations, and familiar yet reverential confidences; if you train your imagination to pasture itself upon all things fair and pure, till your soul becomes a kind of miniature Catholic Church, well furnished and hung round with sacred ideas; if, above all, the image of Jesus crucified is cherished with fervid affection in your heart of hearts; and if, after Him, the name and thought of her who is known as "Mother most pure," "Mother most chaste," are as an all-pervading fragrance, sweetening and purifying whatever they touch: if such be your aim, then you will have a powerful defence against all evil thoughts. If it cannot be affirmed that you will be free from their attacks, it is certain that you will *feel* them to be attacks: your soul, like a sensitive plant, will shrink back and coil itself up into an attitude of fear, indignation, and repulsion; nor will that happen now and then only; or when your attention is pointedly called to what is passing; it is a position of mind which will become a second nature; it will be often assumed unconsciously, and with something of the rapidity of our instincts of self-preservation. As long as you live, imaginations contrary to holiness may rage around you, as the waters of the Deluge swept incessantly around Noe; but fear not: a mind habitually filled with innocent and holy thoughts is a strong, well-enclosed ark, which will find its Ararat of rest when the turbulent voyage of life is over; then will it know, by a blessed experience, what is meant by the promise of our Lord, "Blessed are the pure in heart; *for they shall see God.*"

IV.

SHALLOWNESS IN RELIGION.

"Other some fell upon stony ground, where they had not much earth." *Matthew* xiii. 5.

THE ground here described as "stony" had not been trodden into hardness by the feet of passers-by, nor was it exposed to such accidents as those to which a public wayside would be liable. It was unfitted for seed because it was stony underneath the surface. The ground consisted of a shallow layer of earth covering a base of rock. A person who judged hastily, from appearances alone, might easily imagine that the seed had found there a very excellent home. This conclusion, however, would turn out to be a mistake; for, when driven within the soil, the spade would soon be felt to strike on a flinty substance. The consequence was that the suitability of that ground for seed was very imperfect; it looked well on the surface, for the stone or rock was hidden underneath; but when the seed, after springing up for a time, endeavoured to strike deeper—when it wished to push below as well as above—then the real state of the case was discovered. The rocky nature of the soil was a barrier to the seed, which wasted its strength in vain attempts to strike roots that would hereafter produce the full ear of corn. The seed battled for a while bravely with its difficulties; but there was no reserve of moisture to refresh its languishing strength; for the rock could not hold the dew or the rain, and the sun with its fiery beams scorched the tender shoots that had sprung up at their first contact with the earth. So the seeds, good and teeming with an inner life as they were, and fresh from the hands of the careful and anxious sower, gradually pined away into death. "Because they had not root," said our Lord, "they withered away." All the most watchful attention in the world could not have saved that seed: it was still in the ground; for, unlike that on the wayside, the birds of the air had not consumed it; but it was in the ground only to give false hopes to the sower: it was there to disappoint, and not to give joy. Nor could anything have made it fruitful: even if the burning rays of the sun had been deadened, even if an industrious hand could have watered it daily, even if well-fenced and well-watched, still it could not have survived. Death was written upon it from the first: the soil was its grave, not its cradle and resurrection; its early shoots were a mere flickering of life, and nothing more; for it was rootless, and therefore withered away.

Let us now see what practical lessons we can learn from this part of the parable. In the first place, it condemns at once all those whom we may call half-and-half Christians. If anything be plain in the revelation of God to man, if anything be plain in the teaching of Jesus Christ, it is that true religion claims from us our entire submission and our undivided love. "He that believeth" (namely, whatsoever things I have revealed) "shall be saved;" and "He that believeth not" (everything which I have commanded to be taught) "shall be damned." There is to be no half or quarter faith, but a complete undoubting obedience of the mind. So with the will. "Thou shalt love the Lord thy God with *all* thy heart, and with *all* thy mind, and with *all* thy soul, and thy neighbour as thyself." "He that putteth his hand to the plough, and looketh back" (that is, as if uncertain whether he shall go on or not with the laborious work of the plough—namely, the sanctification of his soul), "is not worthy of being called My disciple." When a certain man came to Jesus asking to be allowed to go to his father's funeral before following our Lord, he received this decisive answer: "Let the dead bury their dead; follow thou *Me*." "He that loveth father or mother, wife or children, *more than Me*, is not worthy of Me." "Not everyone that saith, Lord, Lord, shall enter the kingdom of heaven; but he that doeth the will of My Father, Who is in heaven." These passages, and many more might be quoted, all show that the Gospel of Jesus Christ is intended to draw to itself our whole being. It is not, as some imagine, a creed only, or a devotion that may be intermitted, a temporary service, or a pious diversion, good for some days of the week, and not for others—good, as teaching a right faith, yet not essential as a guide for our whole conduct in all the concerns of our daily behaviour. No; St. Paul's words express what Christianity is when he says, "To me *to live* is Christ." You know that life is a power, a force, a current which circulates through every nook and cranny of our body: we cannot have one arm quite dead, and another quite alive; we cannot have the brain working vigorously, and the heart perfectly still. So it is with Christianity: Jesus Christ is to live and dwell in every part of us. As He filled His sacred Manhood with His Godhead, and as He did not visit for a time that Manhood, but became rooted in it everlastingly, so His kingdom is like Himself. "Let *the same mind* which was in Christ," says St. Paul, "*be in you.*" The same mind in you! St. Peter describes the Christian as a "living stone built up into Jesus Christ—a holy house;" and St. Paul prays for his disciples, that they may not receive the grace of God in vain, but may "walk in it," as a man walks in his body, or in a path.

Our Divine Saviour therefore expects all of us to receive Him entirely; we are not to let Him have one foot only on the threshold, or keep the door of our soul partly closed against Him. We are not to obey one of His commandments and disobey another; we are not to pick and choose between the inspirations of His grace, admitting some and declining others. We are not to attempt to obey Him only by a partial service, so as to *dissolve* or loosen Christ, as St. John expresses it; thus in spirit imitating the cruel soldiers who desired to break the limbs of our Lord. No; Jesus Christ will not come to us on these terms: He is to be *our All* or nothing; He is to be our absolute King, and not our constitutional sovereign or our servant. He has given Himself for us, that we may give ourselves to Him. As He united Himself truly with our humanity, so the spirit of Jesus must spread through all our dealings with God, with ourselves, and our neighbours. St. Paul expresses the doctrine in a beautiful figure: we are, he says, the savour and good odour of Jesus Christ. As that which has been steeped in some sweet fragrance reminds us of that which has touched it, and we think of nothing but the fragrance, so the will of Jesus must so completely steep our hearts in itself that all who know us shall be infallibly reminded that we have "been with Jesus." Who, then, is the half Christian represented by the stony ground? It is the man who will take the Gospel for his rule as far as it suits his inclination or his earthly interests, and desert it the moment it interferes with these interests. It is the man who will be kind enough to those whom he likes or who are useful for his purposes, but who will keep hatred towards his real or supposed enemies locked up in his breast, as though it were a treasure to be prized and guarded, when it is weighing down the balance of God's justice against him. It is the man who has a large vocabulary of pious phrases ready at hand, and is fluent in excellent professions and promises, forgotten as quickly as they were uttered, and never from the first intended to be fulfilled in the face of the slightest difficulty. It is the man who is in private life blameless, and yet who thinks that, in dealing with the public, gross and extensive cheatery in commerce is not robbery, but only a useful sharpness which is a credit to his skill. All these characters are half Christians; they allow our Lord to go to a certain depth in the soil of their hearts, and then they meet Him with their selfish views, their bargains and conditions, and their earthly interests. Jesus, in His love, wants to sanctify all their nature, and they will not allow Him. He feels eagerly for ground to root in them His graces, and behold, He is met with some miserable pretext of policy: it does not suit them to be too good; it will not pay to be complete Christians; they want a little of the Gospel and much of the world; they want to divide the kingdom between self and Jesus; they want to be half rock and half soil. But what becomes of the seed? What becomes of grace? What becomes of their hope of salvation? Having no root, Jesus Christ withers away in their hearts.

"They sprung up immediately, because they had no deepness of earth." These words are full of warning on the deceptiveness of a superficial religion. First, it is a warning to the young. In youth there is much more feeling than serious thought; as there is a certain freshness, quickness, and buoyancy in young blood, so there is much emotion and gush of sensibility. The young love easily, and dislike easily; excitement and change form a great part of their pleasure; and the things which they do not love are, obedience to rule, order, and perseverance; anything fixed is a yoke; they are perpetually craving for liberty. Here, then, is their special peril. The danger is, that their religion will have in it much more of feeling than solid love; they will naturally prefer those duties which fit in with their desire for excitement, to those which demand self-denial and regulation of their passions. Kept carefully, as many are, in the bosom of their families, with few temptations and no experience of the world, it seems very easy for the young to be Christians. We are not now in the terrible days of martyrdom, when, like the Holy Innocents at Bethlehem, young boys and maidens were torn from their mother's side, and forced to walk through blood to the gates of heaven. Matters are comparatively smooth for young Christians in these days; the testing trial comes later; the martyrdom assumes a different shape. When they find themselves face to face with strongly exciting temptations, when the world proves more disappointing and more wicked than they had imagined, then it is seen whether their love to God has had any real root in their hearts. My young friends, be careful to examine your souls. You think you love Jesus. Are you, then, obedient at home to your fathers and mothers? are you quarrelsome with your brothers and sisters? are you vain of your looks or your dress? are you willing to come to Mass and Benediction at some inconvenience? are you modest in all your actions, in private as well as in public? are you lovers of truth? do you pray with attention and fervour? These are some of the questions I advise you to put to yourselves. If when young you lay a solid foundation of holy habits, the probability is, that your gray hairs will be to you "a crown of glory;" but a careless frivolous youth too often ends in a hardened and impenitent old age.

This parable, also, should be a lesson to those who are new converts to the Catholic Church. A conversion is like a first love; everything at the beginning is fresh and blooming; it is a change from darkness to light; the new doctrines and devotions are exciting to the imagination; and as the mind grows into the Catholic mould, and the new glories of the kingdom of God open out, there is a warmth and a thrill never before experienced. The heart feels a freedom it never knew till now, and it rejoices like a young eagle in its first flight. In course of time, however, things become more familiar; the newness, and poetry, and gloss wear off. The convert has no visions and revelations and ecstasies: he has to go to confession like anyone else; he has to fight with sin; perhaps his temptations even increase, because the devil is now more busy in trying to destroy him than before, when he saw him quietly drifting through heresy into the abyss of final woe. If he has laid up the Catholic faith truly in his heart, if he has endeavoured to conquer his self-will, if he has made the love of Jesus his leading motive, then the "word of the kingdom" will have taken root in him, and Jesus will gather his soul into His eternal garner. But if his conversion has been of the head rather than of the heart; if he does not mind being a Catholic as long as his path is easy, but frets under the yoke, should troubles come on account of the faith,—then, alas, the seed has been sown in stony ground. He has "no root in himself but only for a time;" he is a convert to the Catholic Church rather than a convert of Jesus; he has come into the Garden of Eden to enjoy the fruit-trees and the flowers, and not to obey God rather than Satan. Difficulties show whether the soil is deep or shallow; they search into and turn up the earth;

so, as Christ says, "when there ariseth tribulation and persecution *because of the word*, he is presently scandalised." Alas for those converts who are guilty of being thus offended! Alas for those whom the grace of God has brought into the true fold, and who, after all their professions, and joys, and first fervour, turn their backs upon their King the moment they begin to feel the pricking of that crown of thorns, which all disciples of Christ must wear, if they are to follow Him into glory! "Through many tribulations we must enter into the kingdom of God," was the warning given by Paul and Barnabas to their new disciples (Acts xiv. 21).

The seed springing up quickly, because there is little soil, is also a figure of a shallow repentance. When St. John the Baptist was preaching in the desert, he exhorted the people to bring forth "fruits *worthy* of repentance." St. John asked for a solid change of life, a change for good, which should be at least equal in degree to their former life of sin. St. Paul says to his disciples, "*As* ye have yielded your members to serve uncleanness and iniquity unto iniquity, *so* now yield your members to serve justice unto sanctification" (Rom. vi. 19). Mere thoughts, however alarming, about death and judgment, are not repentance; mere feelings, however acute, about the misery of sin, are not repentance; mere desires of amendment, however fervent, are not repentance; nor are resolutions, however frequent. We know, by bitter experience, what a wide distance there may be between the momentary shaking of the soul and actual conversion. Felix trembled on hearing the Apostle Paul preach about "the judgment to come;" yet he remained in his paganism. Pharao was alarmed at the miracles of Moses, and made promise after promise; yet, when the plague stopped, he recovered courage, and grew hardened again. Balaam was staggered when he beheld the flashing of the Angel's sword, as he was riding on his ass; but the love of gold drew him on nevertheless. When a Mission was given in this church, I have no doubt that real fruits of repentance were gathered by Almighty God.

Many flung off their spotted garments of evil habits, and have since walked in the way of true holiness; many rose up from the pit into which they had fallen, and have not again been inveigled down by the devil.* But is it not true that with some of you the effect was only short-lived? Like the seed in the parable, your hearts leaped up at the word of the preacher; you felt vile in your own eyes; you cried out for pardon; when you heard of the trumpet of Judgment and the eternal sentence, you shuddered at the fear lest you might be found among the goats instead of the sheep; and when you were told of the sweet mercy of God, and of Jesus waiting like the Good Shepherd to embrace you in His love, you shed warm tears of sorrow and of joy; you made promises —how fervently!—never more would you drink to excess, you said; never more would you go with evil companions, never more would you stay away from the holy Mass, never more would you corrupt your little ones by your out-

* This sermon was preached not long after the close of a Retreat.

bursts of imprecation, and words of double meaning. There was a run upon the Confessionals, and more pledges were given and promises of amendment made in a few days than had been given in a whole year before. Many, thank God! have been faithful; in them the seed of repentance has struck root deeply, and their homes are better and happier. But, alas, it has been different with others! They are to be found as usual in their old haunts. Once or twice they came to confession—they have never been since; once or twice they came to the Altar, and they have never had any hunger for the Bread of Life since. Why, let me ask, do those amongst you, to whom so sad a description applies, thus disappoint Almighty God? Why did you make the good Missioners hope you were spiritually quickened, when it was only the momentary stirring of the sluggard whilst his bed was being shaken? Why have your alarms of conscience, and your pledges, ended in nothing solid? It is because you have taken no pains to have these feelings deeply established within you;

you have not carried them out into practice; you have not changed your old ordinary life one single atom; you have let your liquid iron cool, without running it into a mould when it left the furnace, and so the heat and fervour of your heart have been wasted. Yes, it is a certain truth that our feelings of remorse for sin, our awakened alarms, our longings for something better than evil, must be turned to some practical account, or we shall never truly repent. To be terrified at the thought of the past will be useless, unless we change our conduct for the future.

"Remember Lot's wife" (Luke xvii. 32). At first, Lot's wife was terrified on leaving the cities of the plain; she, doubtless, hurried on faster and faster when she heard behind her the booming roar and crashing explosions of the avenging thunder; she gasped desperately for breath, as the sulphurous air, spreading around her path, began to threaten suffocation; the whole sky before her, reddened as it was with the glare of the fiery rain pouring upon the devoted cities, seemed nothing but a vast furnace without bounds. The rocks were fire, the trees were fire, the streams, the clouds, all were but various forms of fire. By degrees, however, she grew more familiar with the terrible sounds and sights; her heart beat more leisurely when she found herself travelling safely onwards. At length she became bold enough to risk the chance of breaking the strict command that had been given to her "not to look back." She swayed a moment to and fro between conflicting motives; but the magnet of the old home was too strong, so she stopped, turned, and looked behind. In a moment she was lost: God smote her with His wrath, and petrified into a "statue of salt" those limbs which should never have halted until she had set foot in the appointed place of refuge. How many sinners follow the example and share the fate of Lot's wife! What availed it to her that Angels had "taken her by the hand" and pressed her to fly? What availed it to her that she had for a short time hurried in the direction of Zoar? She turned back and was lost, after all. So it is with many sinners:

penitential emotions press them on, and Confessors full of solicitude, like the Angels guiding Lot's wife, take them by the hand and cry out, "Save your lives!" "Look not back!" But the Sodom and Gomorrah of past evil habits draw them round with a terrible fascination; they *do* turn back; and then, too often, death coming unawares petrifies them into an unchangeable impenitence, and the final malediction of God closes round them with an eternal shroud of woe which no power either of man or Angel can ever unbind. Resolutions of change, made day after day, only to be broken and then made again; Confessions repeated again and again, with the same sins repeated and multiplied; sensations of guilt, without forsaking guilty actions; condemnations of others for what we constantly do ourselves: these things are not that repentance which will save the soul; they *might* lead to it, they *might* prepare the way; but if they really leave us where we were before, we are no better off than if we had never had these visitations of grace at all. The good seed has cropped up "for a time" above the surface, and then, before striking root, has "*withered away*," and all that remains is the stony ground, unblessed, unfruitful, and therefore only waiting for the final condemnation of the Master of the land, the great Husbandman —Jesus Christ. Let us then all, taking warning from this parable, be earnest in the work of our salvation. "Whatever," says Solomon, "thy hand is able to do, do it earnestly; for neither work, nor reason, nor knowledge, shall be in hell [that is, the grave], whither thou art hastening" (Eccles. ix. 10).

Examine yourselves well, and if you find your moral state to be typified by the stony ground—if you find fixed layers, for instance, of old evil habits, or a general passive resistance to all desire of greater perfection, barely covered by an exterior propriety of behaviour, then rest not until you have broken up, or rather, converted into earth, that solid rock by fervent prayer and well-planned rules, and actions deliberately done, in order to change the bad habits into good. There are certain looser stones also, such as vain and proud thoughts about ourselves, envious little criticisms upon others, showing off the cleverness of our own wit and the sharpness of our lynx-eyed observation, rash off-hand judgments, and momentary sallies of temper—these, which are great hindrances to our improvement as well as to our peace, must be removed. We may love these worthless stones as if they were precious gems, but the seed of holiness cannot flourish amongst them; we must therefore dig them out and cast them away with a generous courage, without repining, being certain that without this labour we cannot prepare a good harvest for Him to Whom we have to give a strict account for every grain of divine seed that has been intrusted to our care. For " unto whomsoever *much is given*, of him *much shall be required*" (Luke xii. 48).

Above all things, let us remember that the only earth in which our root will flourish is charity. As imitations of real soil will be of no use to a root, so nothing short of the love of God and man will nourish and support the soul. And as the whole of the plant or tree springs out of the root and is gathered up together in its unity, so our whole being, not an isolated fragment of us, must derive its force, direction, and harmonious expansion, from divine love. St. Paul furnishes us with this illustration. His prayer for the Ephesian converts is not simply that they may have a little of the love of God; he bows his knees to the Father of our Lord Jesus Christ, that they may be strengthened by His Spirit in the inner man, and that Christ may dwell by faith in their hearts, and that they may be "rooted and founded in charity" (Ephes. iii. 7).

The root of a tree is the chief channel of its nourishment. The leaves, the flowers, and the fruit, depend entirely upon that. Hidden underground, it is the source of the strength, beauty, and fertility which are seen above ground by the passer-by. By the root the tree withstands the storm; by this it remains under the snows of winter alive and erect; through this it draws all those materials which continue its existence and develop its growth. As the root is, such is the tree. Very significant too is St.

Paul's expression, "I bow my knees ... that *you* may be rooted;" not that your faith or knowledge only, but that whatever is summed up in that little word "*you*" may be thus fixed root-like in the love of God and man. The second part of the Apostle's figure of speech conveys a similar impression—" rooted and *founded* in charity." The foundation is to a building, what the root is to a tree. Destroy the foundation, and the whole fabric falls to the ground. However numerous and splendid the columns and ornamental parts are, if the base gives way there is total ruin; fragments may remain, but no building. We must not be content with momentary sensations of love; our constant aim and prayer must be that our whole selves may be, and continue to be, imbedded deep in habitual love. We know the signs of an absorbing love for anything. We are keenly alive to all that has any bearing on our favourite object; it comes unbidden and without effort to our minds; we fear and dislike whatever interferes with its enjoyment. Take, for example, the case of a man with a passion for commercial business. How the idea of it haunts him day and night! how his heart, like the most sensitive barometer, rises and falls with the state of the market! Take, again, the case of two persons who have a strong affection for each other; it seems as if they had exchanged hearts. The love of each for the other is so penetrating, that it colours their whole life; it is the real key to most of their actions. Every word spoken by them has a special force and significance for each other, unfelt and unread by the outer world; looks, which seem commonplace to strangers, are to them mutually magnetic flashes—signals full of meaning. So close is this love sometimes, that their natures are completely intertwined by its web, the slightest shock or tear in one being instantly felt by both. Apply this description of any strong love in general, to the love of God. Does God hold the central place in your souls? He is Alpha and Omega, the First and Last, in His own nature; is He such to you and in you? Do you plan how you can increase His glory upon earth? Do you eagerly seek for intimations of His particular will towards yourselves? Are you grieved if you fall into sin, and rejoiced if you resist temptation? Are you delighted at beholding the fruits of His grace in others? Is the love of God the strongest of all your motives—is it the chief desire that satisfies and yet makes you hunger and thirst for more—is it the most precious of all your treasures? It is by putting such questions frequently that we shall be saved from much illusion; it is by following up these questions by daily correction of our faults and by rectifying our intentions; it is by methodical endeavours after growth in love, that we shall find ourselves rooted deeply in that divine soil. There are some who are quite aware that they are at the present moment very far from anything like this divine love; their daily life is such, if judged by its real motives, that, were it possible for Christianity to be blotted out of the world of realities, they would have to alter little or nothing in their interior. Like creatures that remain at certain seasons torpid with all the chief functions of their nature suspended, so they pass their days; the religious, the Christian, the supernatural part of them being in a state of trance, whilst the mere human will is active. What is frequently their expectation? It is, that when they want to love God—that is to say, when they are utterly unable to enjoy life, or are probably not far from death—they believe that then love will come at their bidding. They have systematically kept their soul barred against it all their life, and now, as though a tide of divine love were waiting to rush in, they think that a little wish will draw the bolt and all will be well. There are, no doubt, spiritual as well as physical miracles in the wonderful tenderness and variety of God's providence. But we have no right to expect in our particular case the one, any more than the other. Grace, as well as nature, has its laws; far more mysterious indeed than those of nature, and beyond our conjecture and calculation; still it *has* them, and they must reflect the unity and order of the Giver. Grace is a "dispensation," a "kingdom," a divine "husbandry." No one can read the Gospels and

Epistles without being struck with the truth, that if the beginning and the end of salvation are grace, yet, without taking certain definite and plainly-taught measures, we shall find ourselves utterly barren of the fruits of grace. "What things a man shall *sow*, those also shall he *reap*," is only one out of numberless maxims that, like some grand axioms in natural science, mirror to us the existence and reign of law in the kingdom of grace. "Thou hast ordered *all* things in measure and number and weight" (Wisdom xi. 21). Not more surely did the seed in the parable of the Sower wither, because on account of the scantiness of the soil it could not strike root, than we ourselves, notwithstanding all our capacities for good, shall wither if we attempt to live without charity.

V.

THREE ENEMIES OF THE SOUL.

"Others fell amongst thorns, and the thorns grew up and choked them." *Matthew* xiii. 7.

THE next kind of soil which our Lord mentions may be described as thorny. Whatever differences may exist between this and the two preceding classes, they agree in producing the same result. They are all fatal to the seed. It meets with various sorts of enemies, such as are represented by the divers kinds of earth, but the end is invariably the same. The seed dies, the fruit of the harvest never appears. Just as one man may be killed by violence, and another be carried off by a rapid disease, and another slowly pine away by a lingering waste of the vital powers, but the end is the grave; so it is with the good seed. If it falls upon any one of the three soils hitherto mentioned, the result is barrenness. If any of you, therefore, after making an examination into your souls, have come to the conclusion that you are safe, because your heart is not hard, or because you have no favourite gross mortal sins fixed like stones in your breast; if you have come to the conviction that you do not fall under either of the two classes of condemned soil already mentioned, you must not for that reason give up the inspection of your soul; for who knows whether or not you may not be found guilty under the third head—the thorny ground? This is far more deceptive than the other kinds, for in this latter case the seed does make considerable advance; it strikes root, it appears above ground, and comes up joyfully and promisingly for a while, but afterwards it is killed. Its executioner, unlike the motionless, passively-resisting rock in the former description, is an active enemy, numerous in the quantity of its aggressive points rather than great in size; it is an enemy which, springing up in all directions, weaves together its forces without much show, and closing its network as it creeps along with steady and sure advance, at length gives a deadly embrace: "others fell among thorns, and the thorns *grew up and choked them.*" By the expression "fell among thorns," we are not to understand[*] that, whilst the sowing was going on, the thorns were plainly to be seen; they had not already shot up and arrived at their full growth, so as conspicuously to cover the entire surface of the ground. When the seed was sown, it fell upon a soil beneath which were the roots of thorns more or less hidden. As the last ground was stony, so this was thorny. The thorns were only waiting for time, in order to be enabled to *grow up.* When the seed was sown, they were in their infancy. They wanted no encouragement, no protection. Just leave them alone, do not interfere with them, do not pull or dig them up, and they are sure to find their way and to prosper. It is amongst these concealed, treacherous, spiky, small yet tough roots and shoots of briers that the seed falls.

Here we have a striking figure of the natural state of all our souls. When Adam was

[*] Trench, *On the Parables.*

condemned, when he fell from Paradise, the earth, that was before genial and innocent, was smitten with a curse; the shadow, as it were, of the first sin moved over it, and it conceived an enemy to man within its womb. "Cursed is the earth; with labour and toil shalt thou eat thereof all the days of thy life; *thorns and thistles shall it bring forth to thee.*" The thorns were to issue forth naturally and spontaneously, and man could have a fruit suitable to his wants, only by keeping them down, plucking them up and burning them, in order that the curse might thus be counteracted if it could not be undone. This curse of the earth, dating from Adam, is an image of our souls after the Fall. Adam's roots of evil are in us. We have certain desires, yearnings, and movements within us, which, if unchecked, if unmortified, if not controlled by laborious efforts of our will under the operation of grace, must inevitably grow up and destroy all that we have received from God. These inclinations are not evil in their own nature, but they incline us to what is forbidden; and if not watched, they will lead us to excess, to lawlessness, to death. Especially we may say of the human passions that they are like wild horses: put them to your chariot without breaking them in, and they will dash it to pieces; break them in well, keep them within bounds, guide them with bit and rein, hold them with a steady determined hand, and they will draw you along in safety.

If you will consider attentively that part of the parable on which I am now commenting, you will see that the danger to the good seed did not lie so much in the mere existence of the briers, for as long as they were in their infancy no great harm was done. The mischief came from their increase: as mere roots under ground they had no power to stifle the seed. When the thorns grew strong and tall and were matted closely together, then it was that they "choked" the seed. Now we are coming to the point of the whole matter. I do not ask you whether you have the roots of evil within you; we all have. I do not ask you whether you have likings and dislikings, whether you have passions and wants; we all have. I do not ask you even whether you are committing some distinct mortal sin, something that you know to be a sin, as well as you know that black is black, and white is white. The parable of Jesus Christ suggests to each one of us to put this question before his mind: Am I following any lawful thing, any innocent good, any honest business, any harmless pleasure, with an *excessive, immoderate,* ardour? This is the real warning about the thorny ground, as you will soon perceive when I call your attention to the words of our Lord. There are three distinct things which He calls thorns. 1. The cares of the world; 2. the deceitfulness of riches; 3. the lusts after other things (Mark iv. 19). Now, considered simply in themselves and apart from our own state of mind, these objects are not evil; they are capable of being used either for good or evil. Take the first, the world. The world—what does that mean in this passage? It means our general life here; it means the kind earth, whose fruits we enjoy; it means the bright sun and the free air; it means the friends and the relatives whom we may lawfully love. The world is each man's sphere in which he moves, to some men very large, and to others very small; to some very splendid, to others very humble. To the artisan, his labour and shop are his world; to the literary man, his books and writing; to the farmer, his husbandry; to the statesman, his politics; to the master, his establishment; to the servant, his position and office under the master. The world is, in fact, that general round of action which every man has to traverse in his daily life. It is the present; it is life, social and industrial. Is this evil? is it a thorn in itself? or is it not rather something in which we all find ourselves by the providence of God? Christianity is not opposed to such a world as I have described. Live we must, and to labour is a duty. What, then, are the thorns of which our Lord speaks? They are the *cares* of this world (not the world by itself), which, *entering in*, choke the word,— the cares of *this* world, not the necessary cares either, but the unnecessary, the immoderate, the over-restless, the imaginary and gratuitous cares. The grand absorbing care of all men must be for the salvation of the soul. No error is so great as to neglect the work of our salvation; this must hold the first rank; about this we cannot be too anxious; this is a work we must carry on "with fear and trembling." The cares of the world become deadly thorns whenever, to use the language of the parable, they "enter in" and usurp that higher business which has the other world for its object.

Like the land in which the good seed was sown, the heart of man is limited. If we give much attention to one thing, this means that we can give little to a different object. There is only one field, and if the thorns are allowed to enter in, the seed *must* suffer in that proportion. "No man can serve two masters; for either he will hate the one, and love the other; or he will sustain the one, and despise the other." Having laid down this broad, undeniable principle, our Divine Master draws the following immediate consequence: "*Therefore* I say to you, Be not solicitous for your life, what you shall eat; nor for your body, what you shall put on. . . . Seek ye therefore *first* the kingdom of God and His justice, and all these things shall be added to you" (Matt. vi. 24, 33). If we do not habitually make the kingdom of God our *first* consideration, then we have no measure by which to determine when the cares of life are occupying too large a space of our time, our attention and affections. Excess means something over and above the proper standard. To settle this, we must have a certain definite idea of that standard which is to rule everything else. If we do not give to the interests of our soul, and the glory of God, the supreme rank amongst our anxieties, then the "cares of the world" will inevitably be in excess; they will rush in like an undisciplined impetuous mob, destroying all distinctions and true proportions. If we are not sensitively jealous about the protection of the seed of the kingdom of God, how shall we know when the thorns are growing strong? Why is it that men and women allow themselves to be so immoderately taken up with trifles? Why is it that they will grudge minutes to prayer or spiritual reading, and think whole hours too short for adorning the person? Why is it that they will lay long and elaborate plans for improving their temporal position, without ever giving a thought how they can correct some moral defect? How is it they will work harder than slaves to make a favourable impression upon those whom they wish to attract, and never consider how they can please the sacred Heart of Jesus by some fresh act of service? How is it that they will sacrifice so much to fashion, which changes every day, and nothing to the unchangeable God? The truth is, that, not having before their minds the real and only great object of life, they have no sense of the monstrous disproportion between the things that occupy them in fact, and those which ought to be their chief aim. Like persons who have a defective vision, or touch, or sense of music, they make extraordinary mistakes, confusing large objects with small, the distant with the near, discord with melody. Their folly reminds us of those unfortunate lunatics, whose whole frame is agitated by some incredible triviality, whilst if the house were crashing over their heads they would not take the slightest notice, or would probably even dance and sing. No man can tell when the "cares of this world"—the lawful anxieties, namely, about temporal matters—are exceeding their proper bounds, and turning into thorns, unless he knows what position the will of God ought to hold in his soul. If we have not seriously settled this point; if we say, "Thy will be done on earth, as it is in heaven," and mean nothing by those words, then we have no safeguard against spiritual suffocation, for we are not aware when the fatal process is going on; we confuse the thorns with the seed; the flourishing of the one with the growth of the other. Thoughts and cares which are really unnecessary, or excessively importunate, are imagined to be duties, or at least signs of harmless activity. Thus, without our consciousness of it, the "throat of the mind" (to use an expression of

St. Gregory) "is strangled by them, and whilst they do not permit a good desire to enter the heart, they cut off the approach of vital inspiration." If this deadly process were always attended with pain, the danger would be less. Unfortunately it is frequently disguised under a form of enjoyment, transitory indeed, yet exciting as long as it lasts.

Job speaks of a class of persons who "counted it *delightful* to be under the briers" (Job xxx. 7); and it is said that the sensation following the beginning of suffocation is often a delicious dream. The brain is stimulated into a kind of sensuous reverie. Alas, how many there are who are full of profitless excitement, enjoying the intoxication of many thoughts, desires, and occupations, hurrying at express speed from one point of life to another, proud at not having a minute of time, as they say, to spare, and yet neglectful of the one thing needful!

There is a familiar optical toy by which a singular illusion is produced. Look into it when it is at rest, and you see certain figures and positions; set it in movement, and not a trace of the original impression remains. As it revolves, new figures and new positions appear that were previously unexpected. All is changed by the rapidity of the motion. Something not unlike this takes place in the minds of those whom I have been describing. If they would only retire a little more into themselves, and remain more tranquil, how differently would they judge of forms and proportions, of substance and shadows! In the busy, restless whirl of their life, all things are distorted, and they themselves are deluded.

After the "care of this world" comes the next class of thorns,—"the deceitfulness of riches." St. Gregory* says, that "riches are deceitful because they cannot remain long with us, and because they do not expel the want of the soul. The only true riches are those which make us wealthy in divine virtues." Contrasted with eternal treasures, and judged by the false estimation in which they are usually held in the world, and by their tend-

* Expos. in Marc. c. xiii.

ency to seduce our corrupt nature into luxury, display, and pride, riches are truly stamped with the brand of deceitfulness. As, however, this world is not evil in itself, but is made evil to us by our misuse of its requirements, so it is with regard to wealth. Gold is not sin; property is not robbery; full banks, paying railways, lucrative professions, thriving shops, or well-stored granaries, are not forbidden by natural or revealed law. The thorn springs with great readiness and abundance out of riches; it is formed, however, more properly speaking, by man himself; riches can only strangle the seed through the fault of the owner. "The *deceitfulness* of riches choketh up the word, and he becometh unfruitful." "Woe unto you rich," our Lord exclaims; "*for you have your consolation in this world.* Lay not up for yourselves treasures on earth, but lay up for yourselves treasures in heaven." Riches are a stifling thorn when they are sought with eagerness, when they are used solely or chiefly to obtain indulgence in the enjoyments of the world, when they so satisfy the possessor as to make him neglect laying up treasures in heaven, when they are spent upon anything except the interests of God, and when, to obtain, keep, or increase them, the rights of conscience, of God, and man are sacrificed. There can be opulence without sin. St. Paul, whilst pointing out the dangerous tendency of riches, does not call upon the rich to strip themselves at once of their goods. His instruction to Timothy is, "Charge the rich of this world *not to be high-minded*, nor to *trust* in the uncertainty of riches, but in the living God, who giveth us all things abundantly to enjoy; *to do good, to be rich in good works*, to give easily, to communicate to others" (1 Tim. vi. 17-19). It is well to bear in mind that it is not the mere *fact* of having abundance, but it is the perversion of that abundance; it is the using it as if we were its real owners, instead of trustees for God; it is an idolatrous devotion to it— "which choketh up the word" of the Divine Sower in our hearts.

Without actually possessing riches you may

fall under the condemnation of the Gospel. A poor room, shabby clothing, and meagre diet, are not necessary passports to heaven. Riches may cast an "evil eye" upon you from a distance. If the thought of wealth excites and disturbs your peace; if out of your rags you inwardly curse the opulent merchant whom you see rolling past in his well-appointed carriage; if you murmur against your humble lot; if you are bitter against those whom you behold rising in the world; if, in a word, you hate the poverty in which God has placed you, as a degradation and an unjust servitude, then it is clear that "the deceitfulness of riches" has cast its spell upon you. Pride, impatience, and a morbid gloating over unpossessed goods are your suffocating thorns. Poverty which is only in the exterior, is nothing worth. "Blessed," says our Lord, "are the *poor in spirit;* for theirs is the kingdom of heaven."

A third class of thorns is enumerated by St. Mark (iv. 19) — "the lusts after other things." This expression follows immediately after "the deceitfulness of riches," and is suggestive of one of the well-known dangers of the delusive character of wealth. Riches pretend to satisfy the soul before they are actually possessed; when possessed, it is discovered that they increase desires that existed previously, and give rapid birth to others that were not even thought of during the absence of wealth. Great abundance is wonderfully prolific in imaginary wants; it peoples the fancy with countless ideas of the desirable, the pleasant, the possible, and the impossible; it sets the mighty machinery of the appetites in movement with an appalling power and constancy; and it has revealed to many a man a capacity within himself for restlessness, ambition, and yearnings of various kinds, of which he had previously neither experience nor even any conception. Riches seldom stand alone; like the noxious luxuriance of tropical soil—the favourite haunt of fever-atmosphere and dangerous insects and reptiles—they are too often nothing but the genial breeding-ground for "lusts after other things." These, although not explicitly mentioned by St. Matthew, as they are by St. Mark, are therefore substantially included in the second class of thorns, "the deceitfulness of riches," as being their usual and natural offspring. The expression "other things," or "the rest," as it may be literally translated, seems, however, to require a wider application; and it will then embrace all things (besides "riches" already alluded to) which man is by natural inclination tempted to seek.

Taken in this larger sense, the expression teaches us, whether we be rich or poor, how fatal to divine fruitfulness are *all* desires except that which is called the "thirst after righteousness." "The lusts after other things, entering in, choke the word, and it is made fruitless."

Deliberate lusts after objects utterly contrary to the law of God destroy the soul at once and directly: they draw upon it a withering blight in a moment. Less obvious, and yet not less certain, is the final effect of unrestrained indulgence in a spirit of craving for things which, although not in themselves sinful, do not aid us in the work of our salvation. For the former we are more or less forearmed, because forewarned; the latter, however, "choke the word" with the same certainty as the first, and with far less advertence on our part. "The word is made *fruitless*" if we are perpetually wanting what we have not got, if we are ever thinking about what we wish to avoid in the shape of pain, and what we wish to obtain in the shape of pleasure. If we are always building ideal castles in the air, instead of securing our house upon a rock, if we are always casting about for change, how can there be in our hearts that humility, patience, and trust in the will of God, without which no soul, however otherwise gifted, can bear "fruit unto sanctification and the life everlasting"? (Rom. vi. 22.)

Be, then, most earnestly upon your guard against these three classes of thorns, — the cares of the world, the deceitfulness of riches, and the lusts after other things. Jesus Christ Himself has marked them as deadly enemies of His kingdom; and who will dare to dispute it? At the day of judgment no man can offer an excuse like the following: "O God, I did not pray as I ought, I did not frequent the

Holy Mass and Confession as I ought, I did not give help to the needy as I ought, I did not attend to the interests of the kingdom of God as I ought, because I was busy with the world, and anxious to be well-off, and desirous of many other things." Such a man must be struck speechless; for the Master of the soil will say: "Did I not warn you that these were thorns? why did you allow your immortal soul to be surrounded by them? Grace and salvation are strangled within you; they are dead; and now there is no redemption."

Be warned therefore, my brethren, in time. Look well into the state of your *cares and your desires*. See which is the greatest *now*—your love of this world or of the kingdom of God; and look into the question like men in real earnest. For these selfish and dangerous cares and lusts come up without observation: as a thorn grows in silence, and strengthens by very gradual degrees, so these worldly desires interweave themselves by stealth into our moral life; they creep one by one, little by little, day by day, hour by hour, into our motives, into our pursuits, even into our devotions. The thorns in the parable killed the good seed, not by piercing the shoots of the corn, but by drawing from the root of the seed the necessary moisture; they prevented the free access of air; they stood between the corn and the sun's genial warmth: then the wheat became feeble and sickly, and pressure did the rest. So it is with those Christians who allow this world to embrace their hearts too much: the life of their religion is drained away by things which have no concern with salvation; their soul sickens for want of the celestial atmosphere and pure light of the other world.

Remember, too, that there is no standing still in this important matter: if the good seed does not grow, the thorns will. If the love of God does not put down the cares of the world, and the deceitful attractions of earthly gain, and the immoderate love of pleasure, then these last will be the conquerors. Being sons of Adam, you have the root of these desires within you; but being Christians and Catholics, the Son of God has sown in all of you His truth and grace. There is no undoing of these facts. Satan is watching for the growth and ripening of his harvest, the harvest of sin here, and eternal ruin hereafter; and Jesus Christ is also watching for His harvest from the same soil, the harvest of good works here, and eternal life hereafter.

In your souls the momentous battle is going on. Now, at this very moment, either the deadly thorns are making their triumphant way, or the seed of the divine Sower. Either the cause of Satan or the cause of God is in the ascendant. The final issue is not over, but the elements that will determine it are becoming more defined. The scales are in movement. O tremendous balance! O mystery of good and evil, that in souls upon whom the dew of the Blood of Christ has been so often and so copiously shed, there *can* be any hesitation, any doubtful strife! Yet there is a balancing to and fro, and a critical struggle, of which the all-seeing eye of God alone can discern the future result; and that result is coming nearer and nearer as the sands in the hour-glass

Q

of life run down. What a choice,—our great "adversary the devil," or Jesus Christ! What an end,—hell or heaven! St. Francis of Assisi used at certain times of the year, particularly in Lent, to retire to the rocky solitudes of Lavernia, far inwards amongst the mountains.* There he built for himself a little hut of boughs, with an opening at the top, from which he could look up at the seemingly-infinite blue vault of his native sky; below him was a deep ravine with abrupt and jagged sides. In this spot, whose silence was only broken by the cry of some wandering bird, or the footfall of the lay brother bringing him a little crust of bread, the Saint spent hours in meditation. And we are told his favourite thought was thus expressed: "Heaven is open above, and hell is open beneath, *and the Christian hangs between.*" The longest time that can be spent in the purgatorial middle region is such a small point when contrasted with the endlessness of heaven or hell, that it can be truly said, there

* Cit. ap. S. Leonardo da Porto Maurizio, "Prediche Quaresimali."

are but two places, and the Christian hangs between.

Would that we comprehended this plain, broad, and infallibly certain fact more than we do! Would that we thought more frequently of the words of St. James, "What is your life? It is a vapour, which appeareth for a little while, and afterwards shall vanish away" (iv. 15). Yet vapour though it be, it is charged with two mighty destinies, and it is now moving in one of these directions or the other. Our life is a vapour in its duration; yet to many it is dense and is coloured with the deceptive fantasies of the present, so that the great realities of the future are unseen.

Just as a thick mist may hide from a traveller glorious high-peaked mountains towering above him, and deep abysses yawning beneath, thus it is that the cares and pleasures of this world too often darken the soul's atmosphere, and heaven and hell, which are always closer to us than we imagine, are shut out from our consciousness, as if they existed not.

If you desire to be neither like the wayside,

nor the stony, nor the thorny ground of which our Lord speaks, but like that good soil which alone brings fruit to perfection, then habituate yourselves to think day and night of heaven, and hell. Riches, power, health, comfort, learning, reputation—all these are nothing ; and if we possess them, they are already vanishing fast. The day is beginning to break, and eternity is ready to open before us; eternity as it really will be, unchangeable and inexhaustible in its glory—eternity unchangeable and inexhaustible in its woe—and you and I are hanging between them at this moment !

Out of thorns did the pitiless soldiers plait a crown of agony for Jesus: it rests with us whether, through the grace of God, we shall vigorously do our utmost to pluck out with an unshrinking hand, though we be wounded in the work, all noxious briers from our heart, and so allow the good seed to grow freely and abundantly; or whether we shall, through malice or cowardly compliance, allow the enemy of souls to weave out of the thorns of our sins another chaplet of cruel ingratitude, and ignominy for our Redeemer. May we escape that awful danger! may we, through the mercy of God, be finally and truly described in the concluding words of the parable: "This is he that heareth the word and understandeth, and beareth fruit, and yieldeth the one an hundredfold, and another sixty, and another thirty"!

THE TEN VIRGINS.

I.

DIGNITY AND RESPONSIBILITY OF THE CHRISTIAN.

"Then shall the kingdom of heaven be like to ten virgins, who, taking their lamps, went out to meet the bridegroom and the bride: and five were wise, and five were foolish." *Matthew* xxv. 1, 2.

WIDELY different as was the final lot of the ten virgins, they all had at the beginning the same object in view, and they travelled together, to a certain distance, on the same road. They had all been chosen for one special purpose, namely, to meet the bridegroom whose marriage was announced to be at hand. Whatever their particular positions might be in life, whether they were exalted or lowly; and whatever their abilities or usual occupations were, they were all equal in one respect. Their sole business, on the occasion of the approaching marriage, was to go forth and meet the bridegroom. Everything about them was to be arranged with direct reference to this work. Were they full of energy, that energy must be turned to account. Had they talents, they must find scope for applying their abilities in doing honour to the event. Their costliest ornaments and fairest garments must be brought out, and carefully put on. Fatigue must be forgotten, distractions must be overcome, so as not to interfere with the main business for which they had been invited. Unnecessary anxieties must be suppressed; and if they had any depressing sorrows, they must be quietly buried in this one thought—we are going forth to meet the bridegroom.

Behold, in the first part of this parable, a striking illustration of this life of ours. The ten virgins travelling together on the same path represent the mingled mass of Christians, good and bad, before the final separation is made. Christians may be appropriately called virgins, because they have been by Baptism solemnly consecrated, soul and body, to God; at the font, they made, through the lips of their sponsors, a protest against the world, the flesh, and the devil; and the Holy Ghost entered their souls to purify them and set them apart as temples for Himself. "I have espoused you," writes St. Paul, "to one husband, that I may present you as a chaste virgin to Christ" (2 Cor. xi. 2). They may, if Catholics, be called virgins also, on account of the faith by which they are kept free from any polluting fellowship with error.

To be virgins going forth to meet the bridegroom suggests, moreover, the high dignity of the Christian vocation. It was an ancient custom of the Jews in the East to select a band of young maidens to go forth and accompany the bridegroom to his home, together with the bride. The office was one of distinction, especially if the marriage was between persons of exalted rank. Their march was a kind of triumphant festival. Every passer-by made way for them as they trooped along. They moved to the sound of exhilarating music in the balmy night, with the stars shining brilliantly over them, and their lamps in their hands symbolical of joy, purity, and watchfulness; flowers were strewed before their feet, and at different points of the line of procession garlanded arches were erected under which they passed. The nobleness of the bridegroom and his bride were the glory of the maidens; and the most insignificant among them was on such occasions more distinguished than those of her acquaintance who had not been invited to the marriage.

The Christian life in its combination of that which is obscure and imperfect with that which is definite and glorious, of fear with confidence, of sorrow with joy, of desolation and abundant peace, is not unfitly typified by the time at which the ten virgins began to move. The marriage was, according to the custom in the East, to take place at night. Is not this a picture of our own life? Notwithstanding all our knowledge, natural and supernatural, we are like travellers journeying amongst shadows. Faith undoubtedly is a wonderful kind of soul-sight. "We *see*," writes the Apostle; yet he takes care to tell us, that however dear and precious this power is, still it is by no means a perfect vision. "We *see now*," that is undeniable; but the rays from the truth come to us through a dim glass. "We see now as through a glass in a dark manner" (1 Cor. xiii. 12). We have the truth of God, but it is wrapped up in a fold only partly transparent. This veil is thin enough to enable us to discern for all practical purposes the general outline of revealed wisdom, but we cannot perceive its height and depth, its qualities and colours. That which we now see is as real as our own existence. It is before us; it is unchangeable; it is the supreme law to our understanding and our will; it will judge us at the Last Day as a measure in the hands of Christ; if all the world rose up every instant and declared it was false, it would ever be true, and "all the world a liar." Nevertheless, in this state of our pilgrimage the holiest amongst us must confess with St. Paul, that although what they, by the grace of God, do discern, is enough at times to entrance them with unutterable emotions, still, the most perfect sight attainable by faith is darkness, if compared with the vision in store for all who shall behold the Truth Himself "face to face."

How little too, after all our conscientious study, do we know of the geography of our own heart—its abysses and shallows, its hidden fires and its winding labyrinths! Still less do we comprehend the hearts of others; strangers, or even familiar friends. How arduous is our forecasting of the probabilities of our future, and how treacherous our history of the past! What miserable biographers we make of the very lives which none but ourselves have lived! what delusive prophets of that which has not yet risen above the edge of our narrow horizon!

Like the virgins in the parable, we are travelling by night. Like them, too, we are engaged in obeying an invitation, the thought of which ought to fill us with a deep sense of gratefulness for an utterly undeserved dignity. Our life may be in many respects very mean; it may abound in disappointments; it may last an exceedingly brief time, sailing like a little bubble for a few moments in the air, and then bursting: still there is one thing great about it, which no accidental insignificance can lessen. We are Christians, and our life is the road to the Bridegroom of the Christian. You know who this Bridegroom is: He is a royal Bridegroom, whose "kingdom is not of this world;" a Bridegroom more than human, more than angelic, for men and angels adore Him. It is Jesus Christ, the God-Man. What a dignity beyond all thought it is, that any creature should have been chosen to go forth through the shadows of this world to meet and to wait for such a Bridegroom as this! Should you be tempted to fancy that your present temporal position is inferior to your deserts, should you be tempted to envy others who are more favoured by this world's smiles than yourself, recall to your memory who you really are. Remember that you have been created and redeemed for one grand object —to wait for Jesus Christ. For this the sign of the Cross was placed upon your brow, like the chaplet on the virgins in the procession; for this the lamp of the truth was given to you, and the oil of the Spirit of the new birth, that you might meet Jesus Christ, first at the close of this life, and then on that great bridal day, when He shall come forth in clouds of glory surrounded by His holy Angels, to celebrate that immortal union which shall have no end—the marriage between Himself and His Spouse, the Holy Catholic Church, then perfect in its predestined number, and "not having spot, or wrinkle, or any such thing" (Eph. v. 27).

Besides exalting us with its dignity, this reflection is a source of no slight consolation. The remembrance that we are on the way to this Divine Bridegroom, and that if we arrive safely, and are received by Him, everything else will seem of little consequence, is a powerful sustainer of the soul in the midst of the inequalities and injustices which may be met with on the journey. Why do men strive and push so hard in what is called the struggle of life? Why are they so impatient, so surly, so embittered, as if everything was in a conspiracy against them? It is chiefly because so few feel satisfied with their present lot; the world at large seems unfair, and each individual grapples and fights doggedly and desperately with it, in order to rectify its supposed inequalities, and usurpations of what he deems to be his natural rights. Yet, when calmly considered from the only true stand-point, how small are all these differences of rank, ability, or fortune! If we regard our life as we ought, we shall endeavour to make it answer the description given by the prophet Isaias of the "way of the Lord:" "Every valley shall be exalted, and every mountain and hill shall become straight, and the rough places plain." This life must be not the way of man, but the "way of the Lord." All the nobility and splendour of this world are absolutely nothing when compared with this one fact, that the King of kings is waiting for us, that we may do Him honour and beatify ourselves. What if we have to toil laboriously for a bare living; what if we are obliged to dwell in some unfashionable street or in a poor cottage; what if those who were once far below us have now risen so much that they do not see us when they pass us by? Let these, and a thousand other inequalities far more serious be our portion for perhaps all our years, what then? Are we not called to something beyond this world? are we not invited to the mystical marriage of Jesus Christ? What are all the distinctions of the earth when set against our election to form a part of the bridal train of our God?

To the Christian who keeps such thoughts as these ever fresh in his mind by meditation and prayer, the hope inspired by them is a root of delight and quiet endurance. "We glory," says St. Paul, "*in the hope of the glory of the sons of God*" (Rom. v. 2). "*Rejoicing in hope*, patient in tribulation" (Rom. xii. 12). This hope is like a clear and soft light shining over a distant and longed-for shore, and casting its peaceful beams over the troubled waves in which the little bark of our life is tossing, seemingly the sport of the billows, but in reality their master. It may be that for a long period, and from unexpected causes, sorrow after sorrow has rolled over the Christian; "the floods have gone over" him. Now, it is the sudden loss of worldly means; now, it is the desertion of those who ought to have stood firm and flinched not in the critical moment when everything turned upon their fidelity; now, it is separation by death from those with whose affection our own hopes and fears and expectations and feelings were closely and most tenderly interlaced. Whatever our trials may be, we "reckon that the sufferings of this time are not worthy to be compared with the glory to come," when we shall behold the King in His beauty. Bitter here are the partings from much-loved relations and kind generous-hearted friends; but even this bitterness will be almost transformed into sweetness by the fervent and solidly-founded hope of another and a new meeting that shall never be interrupted, and a joy that shall never be mingled with disquieting fears lest it should perish. "Moses cried unto the Lord, and He showed him a tree, which, when he had cast into the waters, they were turned into sweetness" (Exod. xv. 25). Such a branch is the hope of meeting Jesus Christ, in the souls of all whose hope is "sure and firm," "a good hope through grace." "Fear not," said Jesus to His sorrowing disciples; "for I will come again, and your joy shall be full." To the faithful followers of our Lord we can truly address the following exhortation: "Forgetting the things that are behind, and stretching forward to those that are before, press towards the mark." If distresses come upon you, say within yourselves, "Never mind; I am wending my way to One Whose ear is ever open to misery, and of Whom it is said, 'the bruised reed He shall not break, and the smoking flax He shall not quench.'" If men shall judge you wrongly, and "speak evil of you falsely," say, "What matter? I am going to One Whose justice shall, at the last day, shield and crown the victims of calumny, with glory." If you meet with contemptuous looks and sharp piercing words, say, "Why art thou sad, O my soul, and why dost thou trouble me? I am going to Him Whose countenance shall beam upon me with a tenderness which 'the heart of man cannot conceive.' I am going from this weary land, called life, to that nuptial feast, called heaven, where the Bridegroom and the Bride shall dwell for ever in unspeakable bliss." Such is the hope, and such might be the words spoken in humility by those who are, through much tribulation, on their way to the kingdom of heaven.

From this consoling thought we now pass on to another, which is suggested by the parable under consideration, and which is full of warnings. If in the parable there be, as in the garden described in the Canticles, "sweet cane and cinnamon," there are also "myrrh and aloes." Ten virgins went forth: these ten went in company; these ten travelled on the same road, and were chosen to form part of the same procession. Yet of these ten, five were foolish; of these ten, one half only of all who had been invited to the marriage, and had been arrayed in white garments, and wore crowns of flowers upon their heads, and were furnished with festive lamps, one half only ever saw the bridegroom so as to be welcomed by him, and enter the doors of the mansion where the marriage-banquet was held. Upon the other half, although they had been originally called to enjoy the same happiness and honour as the rest, the doors were shut. "For many are called, but few are chosen." "God our Saviour will have *all* men to be saved," says St. Paul; but God Himself has declared that "broad is the way that leadeth to destruction, and many there be that enter therein: and narrow is the way that leadeth to life, and few there be that enter therein."

As the ten virgins represent the Church of Christ, it follows therefore that we who are members of that Church must be engaged in the same work in which they were employed. We are all therefore, without exception, going to meet Jesus Christ, the celestial Bridegroom; we are going, moreover, not at some distant unsettled future date, but *now;* every moment we breathe we are advancing on the way. Yonder little child, just lately baptised—is going;

before the feeble limbs are able to bear up and balance the body, that infant soul has started on this momentous journey. That young man, who has just begun to taste of the pleasures of the world—is going. That young maiden, who is distracted with so many vanities, and whose fresh bloom of sensitive modesty is showing signs of fading—is going. That old man, who has at length begun to find white hairs upon him before he has thought of the grave—is going. The healthy, who pride themselves on not knowing what sickness means, and the dying, who are counting the running-down sands of their life by minutes; the priest, who consecrates at the altar, and the lay members of the Church; the busy man on 'Change, and the solitary nun in her bare cell; the king and the beggar; the oppressor and the oppressed,— all are going to meet Jesus Christ. There is no escaping from this magnificent privilege, and at the same time tremendous responsibility. Our several names have been called out by the Angel Guardians of each, and that summons will never be retracted. You and I alike are

on the inevitable bead-roll. More certain than
that the sun will set to-day and rise to-morrow;
more certain than that a stone cast up into the
air will fall to the ground, or rivers flow into
the sea; more certain than all these things
is the fact that the Eternal Bridegroom, Who
is also our most just Judge, is waiting for us
to arrive and stand before Him, at the end of
this our journey. When once we have started,
there is no turning back; you are a Christian,
therefore the bridal wreath is upon you irre-
movably, and the lamp is fixed in your hands.
Onwards you must proceed, and onwards you
are actually moving. This thought is enough
to make the boldest among us anxious. Prepared or unprepared, good or bad, loved by
Christ or already condemned, we are constantly
advancing towards Him. In the midst of our
business, honest or dishonest; in the midst
of our amusements, lawful or unlawful; at
sea or on land; sinners who shun the light,
or saints who illuminate the world by their
example; wolves or sheep;—whatever we are,
Jesus Christ is expecting us. He is behind

the lattice, ready to come forth at His own time. Every thought we form, every desire we entertain, every word we utter, every act we do, freely, is a fresh step on this mysterious road.

It matters not whether we are always aware of this or forgetful; we are really passing on to the final destination, just as travellers in a railway-train or a ship are accomplishing their several stages of the distance, whether they are in deep sleep or are nervously awake.

As the journey is inevitable, so also is the end. We must all at last be in one of two divisions—either with the wise virgins, who were admitted into the joy of the Bridegroom; or with the foolish virgins, who were cast out. At present we form one company, they who will be saved being mingled with those who are to be lost. We meet together in the same social circle; we labour together in the same or similar pursuits; we eat and drink together; we dwell together, and have our identical amusements; there is marrying and giving in marriage; and in the bosom of the same family there are wise and foolish virgins, undistinguished by the natural eye the one from the other. Often there are strange mistakes made by those who profess to be shrewd observers; the wise being taken for foolish, and the foolish counted, admired, and spoken of as wise. It is a merciful "secret of the Lord" that we are not able to foresee the final decision. What dreadful revelations do we thus escape, what agonies of spirit, what shocks and lacerations! A merciful providence it is, which prevents the husband from knowing that the wife of his bosom will be rejected and he accepted; or the wife from knowing that she will be admitted and he cast out; the confessor lost and the penitent saved, or the penitent lost and the confessor saved; and so with all the rest of the living who have close relations of any kind with each other. The hour, however, must come when this general bridal train will be put to the proof. Then will come the sifting of the wheat from the tares; then all lesser distinctions will vanish, and one alone be recognised; then the members of the same family and worshippers around the same altar, and the bearers of the same sacred symbols—medals, or crosses, or scapulars—shall be ranged into two classes, which shall never be again confused—the wise and the foolish.

Let the certainty of this fact sink deeply into our conscience. Woe be to us if we expect to be saved by the blood of our Catholic lineage; woe be to us if we expect to be saved by our barren desires, by the prayers of others, or occasional intercourse with the good, or by the excellence of our religious guides and superiors; woe be to us if we try to shield or hide our defects under the general sanctity of the Church at large! Ten virgins travelled together, and were hopeful of the issue, and five were separated from the rest at the last hour. One thing only can save us, and that is—our due preparation for the Bridegroom's coming. Our *due* preparation: not such a preparation as the careless and irreverent and frivolous may think sufficient; not such as those possess, whose consciences have grown dull and lax, and who are imprudent or dangerously venturesome, or too much preoccupied to be on the watch; but such as we are bound to make by the law of divine justice and the rights of mercy; such as He will be satisfied with Who has invited us to the marriage, and has richly enabled us to have all things ready whenever He deigns to come.

II.

NATURALISM AND UNREALITY.

"The five foolish virgins, having taken their lamps, did not take oil with them; but the wise took oil in the vessels with their lamps." *Matthew* xxv. 3, 4.

THE wise and the foolish virgins are both described as having carried lamps in their hands. In this respect there was no difference between them. Nothing is said about the size of these lamps; nothing about their material, nothing about their figure and ornamentation. The success of the wise and the dreadful failure of the foolish virgins did not depend solely upon the lamps. It is not said that the wise virgins went into the marriage-feast because their lamps were large, and those of the foolish were small; nor are we told that the wise carried lamps of gold or silver, and the others only lamps of brass or pottery; nor that those of the former were highly chased and set with gems, whilst those of the latter were simple and unadorned. The case might have been just the reverse, and as far as the mere outward visible lamp, the foolish virgins may have been better off than the wise.

The lamp was necessary in order to meet the bridegroom with the honour due to the occasion; for without it neither the wise or the foolish virgins would have been allowed to join in the procession. But as in the case of the wise their lamps alone were not sufficient to be their title to admission, so neither were the foolish shut out simply on account of their possession or their want of lamps. The issue turned upon the state in which the respective lamps were, when the virgins were summoned to meet the bridegroom; all depended, for weal or woe, on the contents of the lamps—on the presence or absence of the oil which was required for their illumination.

Each of the ten had her own lamp to herself. Not one of the foolish virgins complained that she had been obliged to borrow her companion's lamp, because her own had been stolen by robbers, or broken by some inevitable accident, or for any other reason. At the midnight hour, when the cry came, each was in full possession of an uninjured lamp. We recognise in this incident a similitude between each virgin's lamp, and the soul of the Christian. We all have our own distinct individuality, and nothing can ever alter or destroy this fact. We cannot part with our soul, or share it with others, or by any act of ours strike it out of the world of being. There are some natures of so dependent and so assimilating a temperament, that they seem to live and move in the personality of others,—they are their moral shadows and doubles; and this is occasionally carried to such an extent, that their sense of their own distinctness is seriously impaired, and, with it, the sense of their own responsibility. It is as if their own nature had become diluted by the daily inflowing of the current of other men's thoughts and habits. Nothing, however, that we choose to do or imagine can take away or dissolve the individuality of our own souls. Each has his one lamp; and this represents the natural faculties of the soul—its power to think, to remember, to understand good and evil, its power to hope, to fear, to dislike, and to love—in a word, the understanding, the will, and the affections. We may observe further, that a lamp cannot by itself produce a light; the metal of which it is made and the shape in which it has been fashioned, however beautiful, cannot throw out one ray into the darkness: it wants for this purpose the pouring-in of oil; the pouring-in, because oil will not spontaneously rise out of the metallic substance. It must come from the olive-tree, or the oil-spring, or some other source.

Is not this a figure of the difference between nature and grace? The soul cannot give forth any light such as will fit the bearer to meet the Divine Bridegroom without confusion, unless it has received the grace of God. "By the grace of God I am what I am," was St. Paul's declaration. "You have the unction from the Holy One," says St. John. Man can do mighty works by the natural powers of his soul. He can discover new worlds in the heavens; he can dive into the bowels of the earth, and interrogate the dumb stones about their qualities and age; he can make the sea, relaxing its ancient and tenacious grasp, yield up its primeval shells from depths which it would have, once, been fabulous to dream of touching; he has unravelled, to a great extent, the mysterious laws of light, and succeeded in piercing, for a moment, the fiery veil of the substance of the sun; he has, by his artificial electricity, almost abolished the sense of geographical space, and enabled far-off nations to speak with each other, as though the wide earth were suddenly transformed into a narrow chamber, where we are told, by a wonderful whisper, of thoughts and deeds that are going on thousands of miles from our own shore. These, and many other strange things without number, can man do by his natural powers. But all these achievements will confer on man nothing worth valuing, when compared with the gifts and the results of grace. There is a strong tendency, especially in our own age, to over-exalt the merits of mere nature, and to forget, or throw in the background, or ignore totally and deliberately, the vital necessity and infinite superiority of grace. Do we not see too many evidences of this in the world? When we find vice easily excused, if the vicious man be only clever; when we find the chief distinctions and rewards of the world given to mere success and ability, whilst real goodness is perpetually passed over and trodden upon as scarcely worthy of notice; when we find an idolatry of earthly wisdom prevailing much amongst all classes, whilst the wisdom of all wisdom, the wisdom of the true faith and of holiness, is neglected, if not despised, as an illusion or a sentiment; —we feel, and ought to feel, that a terrible and deep-seated evil is abroad. "Are these thy gods, O Israel?"

Let the lamps of the ten virgins teach a lesson upon this point. What is the purpose of a lamp? is it not made to carry a light? If it fails to do this, it fails altogether. Suppose, if you like, that it is made of the most costly materials, and the work of a great artist—a

Cellini, for example. If it bears no light, what does the richness of the material or workmanship matter to a man who has lost his way in the dark, and is in danger of falling over a precipice? A lamp of common baked clay, such as the Roman peasants used to carry, would, if it had a light within it, be worth more to that lost traveller than a thousand lamps made of gold, if they contained no oil. That which he wants is light, and to him light is, in fact, but another word for life.

If, then, we have to be provided with a light as well as a lamp, if it must be also such a light as will satisfy the Bridegroom, Jesus Christ, and if, moreover, this lamp has been given to us precisely that we may use it for the purpose of making it carry that light, what will be the condition of those who use their lamps, that is, their souls, for every other object except that of honouring, and preparing to meet Jesus Christ? No man can enter the marriage-chamber of the Divine Bridegroom, if his soul be not illuminated with the grace of faith and charity. He may have the genius of a Newton

s

or a Shakespeare; he may be the wisest politician that ever guided the vessel of the state, and the wealthiest merchant that commerce ever placed among its princes; nevertheless, if his soul be unsanctified, he will be shut out of the kingdom of heaven. He may think and boast much of his lamp, and others may admire and envy its excellence; but the little ragged child that in its simple way prays to Jesus, and "grows in grace" as it grows in years, and the poor man who cannot even quite explain the grounds of his belief, and yet, remembering his last end, strives with a penitent heart to obey God,—these two carry a lamp that will do them more service on their way to the Judgment-seat than if they had all the knowledge and wealth in the world, but were without the saving wisdom of God. "He that rejecteth wisdom and discipline is unhappy; and their hope is vain, and *their labours without fruit, and their works unprofitable*" (Wisdom iii. 11). " She is more beautiful than the sun, and above all the order of the stars; being compared with the light, she is found before it; for after this cometh night, but no evil can overcome wisdom" (Ibid. vii. 29, 30).

As merely natural acquirements of the intellect are not sufficient for the great purpose of our life, neither are those social qualities which are so attractive. We meet with persons occasionally who seem to have every excellence but religion. Ask them for assistance in a charitable object, and their purse opens by a natural instinct; they are full of a philanthropic love, which is ever running over; they are men of the highest moral integrity, and in order to tell a falsehood deliberately, or deceive by a dishonest manœuvre in business, or in any domestic transaction, would have to revolutionise their whole habits of mind; nay, conduct of that kind would shock themselves more than it would shock the circle to which they belong. We meet also with persons of intense family affections — fathers and mothers — to whom any sacrifice is comparatively easy, if it is called for by their mutual love; they live and would die for each other, and for their children: the family is their Paradise; its joys

are the only pleasures they care for; and with
it all duties seem to begin and end. Then,
again, there are characters who have an astonishing fund of animal spirits: their lamp of
irrepressible, sparkling good-nature is always
burning bright; difficulties and troubles which
would certainly depress and discourage other
men of a more reflective and timid disposition, are met by them with a genial shrug
and a light-hearted smile. If they were going
near a cataract, they would laugh and sing
as their boat danced along with the exciting
but dangerous rapidity of the current. These
are persons who, partly from natural temperament, and partly from a lamentable want of
thought and seriousness, behave even in many
trying scenes, as if the whole object of life was
to be as merry as possible; the world is to
them "the house of laughter;" and anything
likely to cast a shadow upon their path is
quietly put aside or adroitly turned, instead
of being faced. Now all the characters whom
I have just slightly sketched have a certain
charm about them, especially when they pos-

sess, like a natural bloom, the agreeable softness, finish, and perfume of courtesy and graceful manners: refinement is a great deodoriser of much that will not, in its essence, bear close inspection.

Such cases as I have mentioned, and they are by no means rare, are apt to mislead and influence us for evil if we do not frequently reëxamine our standard of goodness. General benevolence, domestic affection, amiable cheerfulness, exterior grace, and consideration for others, may and do exist, flourish, and attract, whilst beneath all there is a lamentable want of religion. It is possible to give, as the Apostle says, all our goods to the poor, and yet be without that charity for which God is looking. There may be a love of father and mother, wife and husband, brothers and sisters, and also of fellow-countrymen, and of our native land, without any real love of God; nay, the one *may* extinguish the other. So there may be a joy in our hearts very pleasant to those with whom we have intercourse, because it gives radiance to our looks and a charm to our words; still, if this be all the joy we know or care for; if the joy of prayer, of self-control, of meditation, of communion with "our Father," the joy which comes from our "having our conversation in heaven," the joy, in short, of the Holy Ghost (1 Thess. i. 6) is unknown to us,—we shall be like the foolish virgins. They went forth, no doubt, in high spirits, pleased with themselves and every one around them; it was an honourable and delightful occasion; none of the spectators whispered a syllable of bad omen, and their lamps had been well cleaned and polished. Unfortunately the light that began so well lasted only for a part of the way; their lamps did admirably up to a certain point; they were pleasant for the bystanders to look at; they brought out the beauty of their nuptial garments, making the jewels glisten as the rays fell upon them; and if there was anything picturesque on the road, its form would revive in the passing illumination. But, alas, the light was absent at the very time when it was especially required. "Our lamps are gone out." So it is with the mere natural virtues and accomplishments; they are useful and attractive in the present life; but with its extinction their overrated value also disappears.

We are reminded by this part of the parable of the final uselessness of faith when it stands by itself. There are Catholics whose faith it is impossible for a moment to deny or question. So far are they from having any doubts about any part of their creed, that their perplexity is to understand how others, not brought up in the Catholic religion, can have any difficulties whatever. They not only defend their religion if it be assailed, but too frequently their zeal carries them into violence of statement and neglect of charity. They have a hard task to believe in the possibility of invincible ignorance. To them, all who are not Catholics are either too stupid to see an argument, or too selfish to follow out the consequences when they do see it. They are unable to make allowance for education, and unblamable ignorance. They are not the men to be ashamed of making the sign of the Cross, or of admitting themselves to be Catholics. On the contrary, they will often shake their religious flag in the faces of those who are unhappily outside the pale of the Church; they deal anathemas about, as if a profession of faith was worth nothing unless wrapped up in a strong form of imprecation: instead of treating the wandering sheep with a wise gentleness, and coaxing them into the fold, they rush at them as if they were irreclaimable wolves. They enjoy a hot controversy, and tear their opponents to pieces with harsh words and rash judgments, rather for the pleasure of the battle than for the glory of God. Now these men carry a light of a certain kind on their road through the world; they make the Catholic faith known where it would be sometimes never heard of; they carry it into their workshops, and amongst their friends; they carry it abroad, when they leave their own land for business or recreation. But how often is this correct belief—this passionate and courageous zeal—unaccompanied by practical piety! These strong, fearless, determined controversial gladiators are frequently looked for in vain at the Holy Sacrifice: they are not at their post when the priest requires their services in a real work of charity. They are often tyrannical at home, careless about the religious teaching of their children, and contentious and jealous if they belong to Confraternities: they boast much of their powers of argument; but all their fervour seems to spend itself upon refuting the errors of others, whilst their own heart is left utterly without discipline.

This, again, is a light which will not avail them when *they themselves*, and not others, are called to meet the Bridegroom. The Catholic creed without Catholic obedience will save no man. "Faith," says St. James, "without works is dead"—*being alone*. It is the skeleton framework of religion without its body and life.

This thought leads us on to another. The foolish virgins could not produce light, because they had no oil. The lamp was there, and the wick was there, for *all* the virgins rose and trimmed their lamps. The oil, however, was wanting in the lamps of the foolish virgins, and nothing but oil was then of any use. To ordinary observers, the lamps without oil would have looked much the same as those which contained oil, until they were examined inside, and then the cause of their remaining dark would have been evident. This reminds us of the deceptiveness and the uselessness of a merely outward religion. "My son, give Me *thy heart.*" This is what God desires and looks for. "Obedience is better than sacrifice." As nothing is sinful which does not come from the will, so nothing is holy which does not issue from the same fountain. Religion is not a Chinese exactness in ceremonial rites; it is not a mechanical routine of superficial duties; it is not a taste for the poetical or pictorial side of worship. It is "a reasonable *service.*" "The kingdom of God is *within* you." "The kingdom of God is not in speech, but in power." In the prophecy of Ezekiel, giving a description of the future reign of Christ, it is expressly said, "I will give you a new heart, and put a new spirit within you. . . . . . I will put My Spirit in the midst of you; and I will cause you to walk in My commandments and to keep My judgments, and to do them" (Ezek. xxxvi. 27). What is vocal prayer without the spirit of devotion? only a vibration of the atmosphere, that might as well be made by a piece of metal as by a tongue of flesh. What is the kneeling of the body when the soul takes no part in the act? only a posture of the limbs, that might as well be done by a painter's wooden model. What is the giving of alms in the Church, if the only motive is to avoid singularity, or to be ostentatious of our benevolence? a mere dropping of money from the tips of the fingers, of which the sound is never heard in the treasury of heaven; unlike the widow's mite, which rang clearly and sweetly above, as it fell unnoticed in the Temple below.

Outward propriety in devotional acts and a certain kind of zeal, typified by the Pharisees, are no more, in themselves, deserving of the name of true religion, than the artistic imitation of a living object upon canvas can be called life. Pharisaism did not die with the Pharisees who lived in the time of our Lord. It is to be met with still; and it is well to remember how severely it was denounced by Christ. The Pharisees made much of the letter of the law, but they left the spirit to starve; their profession of reverence for the law was great; they wore it in scrolls fastened over their brows, upon their wrists, and on the borders of their garments; so that they appeared to be a kind of walking volume of the Scriptures, their body and dress preaching silently as they moved along amongst the people. Yet their religion was utterly hollow; it was an elaborate sham, as much dead as those painted corpses of their chiefs and head-warriors which the Indian tribes dress up in showy robes and parade before the multitude, demanding for them the same reverence as if they were actually alive. In spite of all their apparent sanctity, our Lord condemned the Pharisees of His day as hypocrites; that is, taking the word in a well-known sense, they were *actors* of righteousness; and the street-corners, the Synagogues, and the Temple were their stage. Being actors of holiness, they had no more real piety than the player in a drama is a real king, though he wears a crown and wields a sceptre. "Wo unto you, hypocrites; unless your justice abound more than that of the Scribes and Pharisees, ye shall not enter into the kingdom of heaven."

None of us are likely to fall into the coarse, and offensively conspicuous hypocrisy of the Pharisees. We are not likely to blow the trumpet of self-righteousness so loudly, or to angle so openly, as they did, for admiration and applause. We are not likely to boast of our attendance at Church, as they did of their visits to the Temple, or to exclaim with a clear, unfaltering voice, "I am not as other men, nor even as this Publican." Is there, however, no danger of our falling into a more plausible, more refined and captivating self-deceit? The Catholic worship is the expression of the feelings, as well as the faith of the Christian man; "out of the abundance of *the heart* the mouth speaketh." Being not a mere creed nor a conventional system, formal and unelastic, but a living body, penetrated through and through with the Spirit of God, the Church is perpetually manifesting this life in abundance and variety. She is not a new revelation only, like a new fact in science, undiscovered before the teaching of Christianity, nor a new event only, like some fresh circumstance which, by happening, takes the shape of history afterwards: the Church is the "new *man*," transfiguring everything human, sin excepted, as she gathers up its elements into her wonderful unity. Her worship, therefore, is the adoration of God by all the powers of the "new man;" and as these correspond to the double nature of man, who consists of spirit and flesh—the invisible and the visible—it is evident that there is much in her worship in which the senses and the body play an important part. As the Catholic Church, considered in her character as "one body," full of "one spirit," manifests her internal faith and affections in outward expressions, the two being inseparable on account of her very nature, it is not difficult to see that she who "lives, moves, and has her being" in an inward spirit, will have an exterior side capable of a merely exterior imitation. Individual Catholics are *in* the Church, in some sense, more or less perfectly as long as they can truly call themselves by the name of Catholic; they are, however, not *the* Church herself. The Church never divorces the spirit from the letter; sensible form is to her always the sign of the hidden essence; she is perpetually a "great Sacrament," as the Apostle writes to the Ephesians (v. 32). All her devotional acts that can be seen or heard, all her rites and ceremonies, are the language of a pure intention and a fervent soul. It is not, however, the same with individual members of the Church: they can, and do separate the inward and the outward in religion; they can, and do copy, nay, even enjoy and be enthusiastic about, matters which are in their case no sign, no expression, no counterpart of a real internal sincerity. Experience every day brings out this sad fact. Amongst the young especially, and those who have excitable temperaments, do we not find persons very demonstrative in their piety, with little that is practical underneath? There are some who would not miss an imposing service of the Church on any account; who revel in the fascination of vestments, crosses, banners, lights, and music, and are never satisfied with enrolling themselves in guilds bearing a distinctive dress; yet who habitually neglect most vital duties of home, and of their individual life. It is not impossible to find the most intense selfishness, and carelessness about elementary obligations of charity and justice, in certain readers of the lives of the Saints. They like the sensational and poetical wherever they can find it; under the spell of their fancy they believe that they rise from each perusal with a conscious exaltation of their souls; beholding the fiery car bearing the Eliases of the Church into the heaven of mystical and miraculous heights, they almost imagine that they are going up themselves side by side with the Saints whose biographies they are reading. If tears come, they are convinced of the depth of their contrition;

if they are in a jubilant frame of mind, they decide at once that some special inflowing of the Spirit has visited them, and they can scarcely attend to the common things of life, and those plain duties which are to be found in the Decalogue.

The imagination is frequently mistaken for the heart, and the state of the nerves confounded with the conscience; nature thus disguising itself under the appearance of grace. There is only one way of avoiding self-deception: we must make it our constant aim to watch and test our fancy and our feelings; we must see whether we are real working Christians or mechanical figures. "By their fruits ye shall know them." Let us take care that we do not, through heedlessness, or self-esteem, or the preponderance of our emotional and imaginative faculties, make the fundamental mistake of thinking that we have in our hands the genuine fruit of the vine, when the grapes are only a skilful composition of marble or wax.

The difference of conduct between the wise and the foolish virgins, the former taking "oil in the vessels" besides that which their lamps would hold, and the others failing to secure this reserve, suggests to us the generosity of the wise, and the niggardliness of the foolish. The wise treated the bridegroom in the same spirit in which they knew he meant to treat them. He would certainly have everything prepared in a manner worthy of his own dignity, of the occasion, and of his guests. His glory was to be reflected upon them, and their joy was to be drawn from his. So they did not spare their oil; whether he came soon or late, they would be ready with an abundant provision for light. This was the true wisdom of love. Their foolish companions, on the other hand, had no such liberality. We do not read of their taking any oil-vessels with them; they thought that the quantity already in their lamps would suffice. They wanted to have all the pleasure and honour of the feast at an economical rate. Why should they lay in an extra supply of oil? Perhaps they might not require it: if the worst came to the worst, they could, as they supposed, make use of the forethought and generosity of the wise. It is a trait of their selfish and narrow character, that when they find themselves in difficulty, they say to the wise, " Give us of your oil;" *give*—they do not say sell, but "give," as if they wished even then to save themselves expense at the cost of the wise.

These five ungenerous virgins have their counterparts amongst ourselves. How many are there whose whole life is an endeavour to enter heaven at the least possible sacrifice! Disciples of a crucified God, they dole out their services as though every prayer said, or penny given in charity, were so much blood drawn from their hearts. A Matthew left all to follow Christ; a Peter leaped into the sea to join Him on the shore; a Paul " suffered the loss of all things." Far different is the spirit of those whom I am describing; and the contrast is often the most striking, because in matters of the world they are probably noted for liberality. They will be prodigal of food and raiment to their bodies, whilst they keep their souls on a pauper allowance. They will have, and proudly boast that they have, a sumptuously furnished house, and highly-paid servants to wait upon them; whilst they can see, without a scruple or desire of improvement, a shabby altar for the Adorable Sacrifice, and poor vestments for the ministering priests, in the Church which they habitually attend. They like a good business, fashionable accomplishments for their children, a large margin at their banker's, and they will provide in their testament for an expensive burial, with abundance of plumes and hired mourners, and every other luxury that the funereal art can suggest. All is changed when religion is in question. The mere crumbs that fall from their table, the refuse of their time, their attention, and property, are good enough for Jesus Christ. The living who are poor obtain little from them, and the dead cry out from Purgatory in vain; for these Christians are too selfish to apply Masses, too idle to gain Indulgences, and too unmortified to offer any works of penance for the souls of the departed.

They only are truly wise who abound in love to God and man. This is the wisdom of the Gospel — " he that loseth his life shall find it;" this is the wisdom which draws from heaven a return of fresh love—"God loveth a cheerful *giver;*" whilst of all follies none is more ungrateful, or fatal than that of stinting God of His due in the midst of our own abundance and indulgence. Solomon's description will apply to the two classes of liberal and illiberal Christians: "One is as it were rich, when he hath nothing; and another is as it were poor, when he hath great riches" (Prov. xiii. 7). "Wo unto ye rich," is balanced by the following promise: "Every one that hath left house, or brethren, or sisters, or father, or mother, or wife, or children, or lands, for My name's sake, shall receive a hundredfold, *and shall possess life everlasting*" (Matt. xix. 29).

The neglect of the foolish virgins to take oil with them in their vessels is also an indication of the danger incurred by those who are perfectly satisfied with their present spiritual condition. The foolish virgins did not look beyond the moment; they let their lamps take their own course; there was no anxious forecasting or watchfulness; having seen their lamps burn at the beginning, they did not make any further provision. They did not even observe the gradual lessening of the light, as the oil was being exhausted: at length the last flicker was given, and all was darkness. "Blessed are they," says our Lord, "that hunger and thirst after righteousness." "My soul is athirst," cries David, "after the living God; as the deer panteth after the water-brooks, so doth my soul seek after Thee." "*Grow* in grace," writes St. Peter. "Forgetting the things that are behind, and stretching forth myself to those that are before, I press towards the mark, to the prize of the supernal vocation of God in Christ Jesus" (Phil. iii. 13, 14). Very different is the spirit of those Christians who, like the foolish virgins, are not careful to have abundance of oil, or to trim their lamps. Their soul seems, after reaching a certain most imperfect state, to remain utterly unprogressive. Their good and bad habits are petrified in the form which they took years ago. They advance in earthly matters; they increase in experience; they never fix a limit to their temporal successes: everything grows and multiplies for them except virtue. They add no new merit to their actions; no better motives take the place of the old ones; not a single higher aspiration is felt to lift them up above the dead level of their original lukewarmness. What is the result, what must be the result? That in reality they are not stationary at all; they are gradually changing for the worse. In the case of the foolish virgins, every step they took, and every hour that the bridegroom tarried, was so much illuminating strength taken from their lamps. So it is with all who are not anxious to be more perfect. Little by little graces disappear; little by little their feeble desires become weaker; little by little their conscience loses its delicacy of perception. They are advancing in years, and approaching nearer to the Bridegroom; yet instead of growing more ready to meet Him, they are becoming less ready. One of the worst effects of a state of indifference as to our improvement in habits of goodness is, that as we do less than before for God, so we are content with less. Our standard sinks lower simultaneously with our conduct. As the light of our lamp becomes dimmer, we ourselves fail more than ever to perceive the real state of the case; we doze away, and only awake to discover that "our lamps are gone out" beyond all remedy. Just as a desire for food is a sign of health in the body, so a desire for more grace and more perfection is a sign of health in the soul. He who is satisfied to be no better than he is at present—he who tells his soul to lie down and take its rest before it has run the race or fought the battle—carries the sign of condemnation within him. Let us remember St. Bernard's golden saying, "The only measure for the love of God is to love God without measure."* And again, "It will be a great, a very great confusion indeed to us, that worldly men crave after pernicious things more ardently than we do after useful things. They make haste more rapidly to obtain death than we do to obtain life."†

* Tract. de diligendo Deo.
† Exhort. de altitudine et bassitudine cordis.

III.

PREPARATION AND PRESUMPTION.

"And the bridegroom tarrying, they all slumbered and slept; and at midnight there was a cry made: Behold, the bridegroom cometh; go ye forth to meet him." Matthew xxv. 5, 6.

WHEN shall we learn to believe in the shortness of life? The patriarch Jacob called his life a pilgrimage. When Pharao asked him, "How many are the days of the years of thy life?" Jacob answered, "The days of my pilgrimage are a hundred and thirty years, few and evil" (Gen. xlvii. 8, 9). A pilgrimage is a constant change of position, a seeking for, and travelling onwards to a solid and lasting home, without abiding long at any intermediate spot.

Life has been compared to a race: you see the runner start, and in a few moments the course is traversed. There is no stopping, no turning aside to rest; it is a short rapid flight, and then all is over. In the Book of Wisdom our days are likened to the swift, traceless flight of a bird through the air: "Of the passage of which no mark can be found, but only the sound of the wings beating the light air, and parting it by the force of her flight: she moved her wings and hath flown through, and there is no mark found afterwards of her way: or as when an arrow is shot at a mark, the divided air presently cometh together again, so that the passage thereof is not known. So we being born, forthwith ceased to be" (Wisd. v. 11-13).

Shakespeare, as you will remember, compares the life of man to a drama. Men begin it at their birth, and close it at their death so rapidly, that it resembles the coming on, and the passing off from the stage, of actors who only play a part for the evening. For an hour or two there is a mimic world; people move about and talk, and scenes change; then, the curtain drops, and everything is dark and still. "All the world's a stage, and all the men and women merely players." By an ancient Father (St. Gregory) life is described as nothing more than a tedious death: it is called life, but it is so near to death, and abounds in so many pains and wearinesses and failures, that it is only death long drawn out. There are, however, few images so striking, so true, so beautiful, and also so solemnly touching, as the one which is suggested to us by the parable of the virgins. "*The bridegroom tarrying, they all slumbered and slept.*" Whilst they were all still awake, and pressing forward, the bridegroom did not come: they were waiting for him, and he was also, for some purpose known to himself, waiting for them. He was on the road, but not visible to the eye—he was tarrying; and then, when the eyes of all the ten were sealed in sleep, when the voices of both wise and foolish were alike hushed, when the active limbs of all were still, the feet no longer marching, and the hands no longer in motion, then it was that the bridegroom came. "At midnight there was a cry made: Behold, the bridegroom cometh; go ye forth to meet him." What did this sleep of the ten represent? It was a state, observe, common to all: we are not told that the wise were awake, and the foolish asleep; in this respect there was no distinction, any more than there had been in the setting out of the procession. All began to start at once, all carried their lamps in company, the wise and foolish mingled together; and so now all are spoken of as being overtaken by the same event. "The bridegroom tarrying, they *all* slumbered and slept;" all—the wisest equally with the most unwise. This sleep, common to all, is a figure of the hour of death. The whole period before this hour therefore represents life; and as, during this period, the bridegroom, although expected, nevertheless did not arrive, and the time is spoken of as that during which the bridegroom tarried, the parable thus furnishes us with a new illustration of life. The hour when the virgins started is a figure of the hour of our birth, their march is a figure of life, and their sleep at the end is death. If, then, we are asked, What is life? we answer, Life is nothing more or less than the tarrying of the Bridegroom, Jesus Christ.

As soon as a babe comes into the world, be it the child of a pauper or the heir to a throne, one might whisper in its ear, if it could understand: "You are born, you live—that is to say, Jesus Christ, the Divine Bridegroom and Judge, is *coming*. If He had arrived, you would be no longer here." To those in mid-life, full of plans and pursuits, full of health and vigour, the same message might be delivered: "You live in the world, you live among your fellow-men, you live in the midst of your business: Jesus Christ is coming. If He had arrived, your business here would have been finished." To those also who have one foot in the grave, whose eyes are dim with age, and who are unfit for the toil and bustle of active work,—to those who seem to do nothing but expect the closing of their earthly career, we may say in like manner: "Ye aged ones, who still linger upon this earth, and have wept over the graves of many of your old friends, ye are not dead yet, the bowl at the fountain of life is not yet broken, and the silver cord, though becoming frailer every day, is not yet snapped. What is your life? It is now, towards the close of your years, just what it was when you first breathed the air of this globe,—it is only the tarrying of the Bridegroom. The delay of the coming of Jesus Christ, your Master, is the exact measure of the length of your life." So many years, so many months, so many weeks, so many days, so many hours, so many minutes, so many seconds marked by the physician's stop-watch at the bedside of the dying man, are only another expression for so many moments of the tarrying of the Lord.

The parable further teaches us that the tarrying is exceedingly short. How brief it is, even if extended to a long sojourn in this valley of tears, is shown by the bridal procession of the ten virgins. They began their journey in the evening—not in the early dawn, but in the evening; and the sleep and the awakening were both accomplished at midnight. So that the life of all men, wise or foolish, the life of the youngest and that of the oldest, is represented as the little space of time between evening and midnight; nothing longer. Thus Jacob felt his own life to be short, although it reached to a hundred and forty-seven. "The *days* of my pilgrimage are a hundred and forty-seven years; *few* and evil are they." Few, although a hundred and forty-seven; few, that is, when compared with the work that his soul had to do; few for the preparation for death; few for repentance; few for the uprooting of evil habits and the acquiring of piety; few, when compared to the vast eternity into which they led, like the passage of a bridge over a narrow stream.

We know that this tarrying will be short, but none of us can tell the exact moment when it will cease. It is uncertain as well as short. In this respect the wise and foolish were on a level. However superior the wise were in other matters, they knew no more than the foolish when the bridegroom would arrive. This is clearly pointed out in the parable; for we are not informed that the wise virgins were up and awake, whilst the foolish were asleep; the wise have not keener eyes to discern in the far distance the approach of the bridegroom, nor more sensitive ears to catch the notes of the music floating forwards on the air as his attendant company advances; nor does any special messenger convey tidings exclusively to them, of which the rest knew nothing. The news comes to both the wise and foolish at the same time; there was no forecasting of the hour within their hearts, no anticipation which of itself made them prepared: "all slumbered and slept; and at midnight there was a cry made: Behold, the bridegroom cometh." "All slumbered and slept." If you had gazed on the sleepers a moment before, you would have seen no difference in their forms—all seemed equally calm; the arms of the wise were perhaps affectionately entwined with those of the foolish. See, they are dreaming; the wise perchance dreaming of having to go forth to meet the bridegroom, and fearful lest they might be rejected; a shadow of sadness passes over their face, even to tears, at the imagination, which was to turn out as baseless as their dream—it is a dream born out of anxiety, and ending in joy. The foolish, perhaps, were dreaming of the joy they would have when the bridegroom came—in fancy they heard his voice, all sweet and encouraging, "Come in to the marriage"—in fancy they saw their lamps burning with brilliance—in fancy they felt their hearts beat with delight at the magnificent feast to which they were summoned. All was an illusion, which the cry, terribly real for them, scattered in an instant. The suddenness of the awakening of both the wise and foolish is a picture of the unexpectedness of the hour when the soul parts from the body, and is called upon to appear before God. Who can foretell the time of his own death? Who has eyes sharp enough to see the fatal sword before it strikes? Baltazzar was revelling in the midst of a grand feast in his palace, with the wine-cup passing round, and his friends and courtiers applauding, when the finger of God, before unseen, came forth, and wrote in awful letters of fire these stern words: "Thou art weighed in the balance, and found wanting;

this night thy kingdom shall be taken away from thee. *That same night* Baltazzar was slain" (Dan. v. 5).

The Assyrian army, which was proud of its strength and glistening with its burnished weapons one day, lay on the next as still as the ground on which the soldiers had sunk to sleep —it was an army of corpses. "At what hour you know not, the Son of Man will come" (Matt. xxiv. 44).

There is not one amongst us who has not been often shocked by the unexpectedness of the death of some friend or relation. Sometimes the very men who assisted to carry the remains of another to the grave have been themselves carried out the next week to the same cemetery. A mother has before now awoke to find in her arms a lifeless child, that was smiling innocently only a few hours before. A wife has fallen over the body of her husband, struck dead by the arrow of her grief. St. A. Avellino was mortally seized in the sanctuary, just as he was saying, "I will go up to the altar of God."

Preparation and Presumption. 291

Even after long illnesses it may be said that death comes on a sudden; for men become used to sickness; they are often so completely engrossed with their wants, so distracted with their pains, so eager to watch the signs of improvement, so pleased in the affectionate attentions of their friends, that at length the idea of death almost passes away. They have been so long ill, that they have forgotten that this state cannot last for ever; hence, they are startled and bewildered and incredulous when a friendly voice says to them, in the midst of tears, "Prepare to die; for you cannot survive the night."

I was once called to visit a sick man, and I saw at a glance that his spirit would soon pass away. I heard the echo of the midnight cry in the distance, but *he* did not; he looked me full in the face, and said, "Why do you think I am dying? If you would give me a cordial, I should live for years; I do not believe that I am going." I exhorted him to prepare for the last; but finding I could not convince him of his nearness to death, and that he only grew more excited, I left him for a little while, that he might think quietly upon my words. When I returned, he was already before his Maker; the cry had arrived whilst I was absent, "Behold, the Bridegroom cometh; go thou forth to meet Him;" and he had gone!

The parable of the Ten Virgins impresses upon us all, that, no matter who we are, no matter how wise or how foolish, no matter how young or old, no matter how strong or weak we are, one thing is certain—we *shall* all hear the midnight cry of death, and it will be heard when probably it was least expected. The cry was equally sudden to both the wise and foolish. Let us now examine a little more narrowly what this death is which comes so suddenly. Remember that death means something more than the cessation of life; it is not the stopping of the pulse and the stagnation of the blood; it is not the closing of the eyes and the sealing-up of the ears. Although nothing seems so motionless as death, nothing is so active; if we look at the chamber where the corpse lies, how silent everything is! Those

Preparation and Presumption. 293

who enter, tread lightly by instinct; touch the body, and it does not stir; speak, and there is no reply. Yet what does faith teach us? What is life, interpreted by faith? We have seen that it is the tarrying of Jesus Christ. And what, then, is death? It is the going forth of the soul to meet Jesus Christ. The body stays behind, but the soul goes forth; the body is still, the soul is awfully active; the body rests, the soul is doing the most tremendous of all work; the body lies wrapped in the winding-sheet, the soul goes forth, either clothed in the wedding-garment of righteousness, or fast bound in that most awful of all grave-clothes, the winding-sheet of sin. The body is laid tenderly in its coffin, and the name which was borne upon earth by the departed is engraved upon its lid; whether worked in silver, or marked as the pauper's with a bit of chalk, matters little. But the soul has no such intermediate receptacle: it is at once either free from condemnation and in the arms of the mercy of Jesus, although it may be detained awhile from the Beatific Vision; or it is an eternal slave in the chains of misery. Death, therefore, is another life; it is the end of one journey, only to be the beginning of another; the end of a short one, to begin a long one. Death is not merely a separation from the body; it is a separation which is the starting point for a new condition, a new country. Death is the answer to the midnight cry; it is the rising up of the soul, now fully awake, now intensely conscious of what heaven and hell mean, what judgment and salvation mean; it is the obedience to a command which brooks no refusal, and admits of no delay. Hitherto, during life, the Bridegroom has *tarried;* now He is *come.* "Go ye forth to meet Him;" go forth to be examined by Him; go forth to endure His searching gaze; go forth from this little world, where you have lived and talked and suffered, where you have sinned and repented, where you have done good and, alas, evil; go forth to meet the awful and glorious Bridegroom, to meet Him face to face; go forth to hear your sentence—joy for ever, or woe for ever. This is death.

Preparation and Presumption. 295

As soon as the ten virgins were awoke by the summons to go forth, the first thing that occupied their minds was the state of their lamps. To hear the cry, and to examine their lamps, was the act of one and the same moment. This was the first thought with each —and it flashed through their minds like lightning: "Then all those virgins arose, and trimmed their lamps." What anxiety there would be in that moment! how each heart would beat! how fear and hope would struggle together! how much hung upon that inspection! for the bridegroom was at hand, and waiting. If the lamps were brightly burning and were well supplied with oil, then all was well, and the rest of the journey would be joyous. Then they might be sure of the bridegroom's smile: then they might anticipate with certainty the welcome salutation, Well done, thou good and faithful virgin; enter thou into the joy of the bridegroom. But what if, through carelessness or any other fault, the lamp was without a light and without oil? A virgin going to meet the bridegroom with an extinguished lamp would only carry in her hands her own condemnation. She need not speak, for the darkness of the lamp she carried would tell its own tale. Of the ten virgins, only five trimmed their lamps with confidence and joy; the light which shone forth upon their radiant countenances being a true figure of the peace within: the others gave a look, and were alarmed. Full of a torturing anxiety, each turned her lamp round and round, but she found only a burnt-out wick: the lamp was still there, mocking, as it were, at her confusion, and silently complaining that it had not been fed with oil and kept burning like those of the others. Then, with a kind of wild useless despair, asking for what they knew was impossible, they say to the wise, "Give us of your oil, for our lamps are gone out." But the wise said, "Nay, lest perhaps there be not enough for us and for you: go you rather to them that sell, and buy for yourselves."

The sudden cry at midnight is, as I have explained, a figure of the shortness of life and the call to Judgment; and the rapid examination of each virgin's lamp by herself is the soul's inspection of its own self. There is no escape from this examination; for the instant the cry comes, "Go forth to meet the Bridegroom," the soul of the departed beholds itself as though it were looking into the glass of Judgment. How often in life do we shrink from lifting up the mask of our own heart! how fond we are of putting-off self-inspection! how much we prefer the favourable and flattering opinion of others to a knowledge of our interior! how we are tempted to call white that which is really black! In the hour of death we *must* look at ourselves: the soul *cannot* turn its back upon itself. The time of concealment is over, for "there is nothing hidden which shall not be revealed." The time of delay is over, for the Angel of God has struck the last hour; and as the relations who stand weeping by the bedside look at the clock in the room, and say, "Mark the time to a minute, for he is dead," at the same instant the soul of the dead looks into its real self, and sees its real destiny. Even for the good, who have been carefully examining their consciences daily, such a moment is a tremendous hour: for eternity is within it; heaven and hell are contained in that one moment. What, then, shall it be for those who find that up to that time they have been deceived? what shall it be in the case of those who were hopeful, and almost certain of salvation during their life, and then suddenly find the end of this life of theirs to be only the edge of a fathomless gulf, on which they stand for a moment, just to see that there *is* a gulf, and are then cast down? Startling as is a sudden death, nothing can be so startling as a sudden discovery that the soul is lost. Who can imagine the piercing shriek of a soul which perceives itself empty of grace, empty of hope, empty of love, just when it is summoned to go forth to meet the Bridegroom? The life of such a man has been only a dream—a dream of security, a dream of religion, a dream of the marriage-feast in heaven; and the hour of death is the hour of his awakening—to find his soul empty.

This is certainly one of the most impressive lessons of the parable—the possibility of being deceived as to our eternal salvation up to the last minute. For the five foolish virgins never seem to have had any anxiety or fears; they laid themselves down by the side of the wise and went calmly to sleep—just as the saved and the lost often lie in the same grave—and never does any suspicion appear to have crossed their minds of their unprepared state until they were aroused by the midnight cry. They never found out, until it was too late to remedy the evil, that their lamps were extinguished. "Give us of your oil; *for* our lamps are gone out," was evidently an exclamation of alarm. Had they been alarmed before they went to sleep, they might have obtained oil: their thoughtless confidence was their ruin. Their anxiety came too late, as the answer of the wise virgins declares, "Go ye rather to them that sell, and buy for yourselves." They are words of reproof, words of hopelessness, words which abandon them to their well-deserved fate. Where, indeed, was the oil to be bought? Where were the sellers? where was the money with which to buy? was it not deep midnight? was not the bridegroom close at hand? Time, means, and opportunity were hopelessly gone.

So it will be with all of us, if, at the hour of death, "our lamps are gone out:" then, it will be too late to undo the past; then, our companions who are saved will have to leave us for ever, as the wise were obliged to part from the foolish; then the evil spirits, who will surround us at that moment will mock our despair with the bitter ridicule, "Go to the sellers to buy for yourselves;" then we shall lose all possibility of seeing the Bridegroom, for "while the foolish went to buy, the bridegroom came; and they that were ready went in with him to the marriage, and the door was shut." "*They that were ready* went in;" not they who had been invited, for all the ten had been asked to come to the marriage; not they who wished to enter, for all wished; not they who thought themselves prepared. The words of the parable are unmistakably clear: " the bridegroom came, and they that were ready went in." That is to say, they that were really ready at the moment of the Bridegroom's arrival. A past readiness, or a possible future readiness, if more time had been allowed to become ready, would not be sufficient. Remember that death can only come once. "It is appointed unto man once to die, and after this the judgment" (Heb. ix. 27). Death is not more sure than that we can die *only once;* we cannot become perfect in dying by any practice or repetition; we cannot rehearse the momentous act; when it comes, it is the first and final reality.

Many Christians have been ready in former periods of their life, who, by falling into sin later on, will be not prepared at the hour of death. How many are there who would have been in heaven, had they gone from their mother's side in their infancy, but are now in hell, through the unrepentance of their riper years! How many were once ready, when the pressure of conscience was upon them, and their hearts were tender, during their first serious illness, yet whom death has found with their lamps extinguished! Those only can go in to the marriage who are actually ready at the time of their summons; even a minute may make an awful difference, for an evil thought indulged in will ruin a dying man, who might have been saved but for that minute's guilt!

We cannot too often ponder over that momentous word *"ready."* For such is our lightness of mind, and so reluctant are we to believe that *we* individually can ever be lost, that we are constantly in danger of being destroyed through thoughtlessness. If there is one thing which is less open to what we call *chance*—one thing more than another which is only obtained by means equal to the end—it is salvation. Has not God Himself worked out the most stupendous plan for its accomplishment? What are the Incarnation, the Death, and Resurrection of Christ, the ministry of Saints and Angels, and the wonderful machinery of grace in the seven Sacraments, but proofs that the saving of a soul is the result of order, law, and system? There was no way of entering the room of the marriage-feast in the parable except by being ready for the Bridegroom. Violence could not force an entrance, nor cunning slip in unawares; it was not an unguarded door, where any one might walk in and take his chance of a seat at the table. No one could enter except he was admitted by the Bridegroom himself, and unless the Bridegroom was satisfied with his fitness. Neither natural virtue, nor our misery if we are shut out, nor our thoughtlessness, can constitute any claim to be admitted. Folly did not save the foolish virgins; it was just their heedlessness which was their crime. They, therefore, who leave their souls to chance, and who imagine that in some unknown, unrevealed way they will, after a life of worldliness and carelessness and sloth, lie down in sin, and then suddenly awake up with a golden ticket for the marriage-feast in their hands, with "Enter" engraved upon it,— such persons will be awfully deceived. The door of the festival-room is sprinkled with the Blood of Jesus. He alone can take in the souls for whom He has died. He is the very door itself. "*I* am the door," are His own words; and He will take in none who are, in His judgment, unfitted for that great bliss. "They that were ready went in *with him* to the marriage."

When the wise virgins had gone in together with the Bridegroom, the parable declares, in simple yet most expressive words, that "the *door was shut.*" Until the Bridegroom arrived, it had remained open, in preparation for those who, being ready, were to accompany him to the feast; but as soon as the Bridegroom came, the door closed. What does this circumstance represent? It is a figure of the two stages of a soul. The first stage is the period during which there is time and means to get ready for death and judgment. It is the season of grace, the interval of invitation, the opportunity for pardon and the Sacraments. During this period the door of eternal life is open, divine love keeping it wide, and divine condescension tenderly beseeching every one to prepare and enter at the appointed hour.

The second stage is that point of the soul's history when the hour of trial and opportunity finishes, and the final destiny begins. Henceforth all is fixed; there is no more passing to and fro, from a state of grace to a state of sin, or from sin to grace; no more fluctuations between heaven and hell; no more going in and out of the fold of the chief Shepherd—to-day a wolf, to-morrow a sheep. The door, so long allowed to remain ajar, is now shut.

Observe, there are not two doors, but *one:* so that the very door which encloses the Bridegroom and the wise virgins is the same which shuts out the foolish. Does not this show to us that the same law which admits the wise is that which condemns the foolish? Does it not teach us that if one soul is saved, and another lost, it is because the same holy justice of Jesus Christ which crowns the obedient, also punishes the wicked? The expression of the parable, "*the door was shut,*" seems to suggest to us that the closing was not an arbitrary act: we are not told that it was the Bridegroom himself who closed it; it closed simply because on the arrival of the Bridegroom, it was not fitting that it should remain any longer open. Thus it is with the condemnation of those who are lost. Jesus Christ has made a law, He

x

has given us all a clear knowledge of what is required for our salvation; and if we are "shut out," it is not so much the personal act of the Judge as the official execution of His law. Death is the closing of the door; and they who at that moment are not ready, find themselves by their own fault outside the marriage-feast.

The concluding words of the parable show the utter hopelessness of the condition of those who are unprepared to meet the Bridegroom when He comes. The foolish virgins are represented as crying out before the closed door, "Lord, Lord, open to us." The darkness outside, and the knowledge of the joy of those who are within, torture their minds. "Lord, Lord, open to us;"—as much as to say, "Do you not see who we are? We were invited by you to the marriage-feast; we are not strangers passing the door by chance; we belong to that procession of virgins which started together at sunset; you know all our names; we are miserable with fatigue; the darkness oppresses us, and wild-beasts are prowling around. Lord, Lord, open to *us!*" But the fatal door moved not; the only answer they heard was one which doubled a thousand-fold their sorrow. "He answering said"—*He*, that is, *the Bridegroom*—it was no servant, who might possibly make a mistake—"*He* answering said, Amen, I say to you, I know you not." There was a time when He did know them; for He had prepared a feast for them, He had furnished them with beautiful lamps and bridal robes, and invited each virgin by name. But their carelessness, their unreadiness, their sloth, their fickleness, their selfishness, had changed the Bridegroom's love into just wrath. "I know *you* not." The wise I know still, and shall love always; they have finished their fatiguing journey, and have left the chilly midnight air and the gloomy solitude of the road, to enter with me to the marriage-feast, where there is nothing but joy and peace and light. But *you*, with your lamps "gone out," I know not; you are only fit for the darkness and the outside of the marriage-feast; you did not get ready for Me before I came; you are not fit to be with Me now that I have arrived.

So will it be with those unhappy Christians who shall die unprepared.

In vain will the lost soul cry out in agony, "Lord, Lord, open to *me!*" In vain will it say, "Was not I invited to the eternal banquet? was not I entered at the baptismal font as one of the bridal procession? do not I bear the name of Christian? have not I had once the oil of the Holy Ghost in the lamp of my soul? have not I been sprinkled with the Blood of the Lamb? have not I believed in Thee, O Lord, and prayed to Thee, and sung of Thee? have not I received Thy sacred Body to support me in the desert of life? Lord, open to *me;* me the Christian, me the Catholic, me the Communicant, me whom in mortal sickness Thy own priest anointed and prepared, as he said, for death." Alas, if that Christian did not die truly prepared by true penitence and true charity for the Bridegroom, he can have but the same answer as the foolish virgins. The Saviour to Whom he has appealed will be compelled to reply, "Amen, I Who died for thee, I Who have loved thee eternally, I Who have given thee graces without

Preparation and Presumption. 309

stint, say to thee, I know thee not. I know what I have suffered for thee; I know the mark upon thy soul, for the print of My Blood can never be wiped out; it will go with thee into the 'outer darkness.' I knew thee when I cleansed thee from original sin; I knew thee when I pardoned thee so often in the Sacrament of Penance; I knew thee when I fed thee with My own Body and Blood, strengthening thy weakness and glorifying thy nothingness with My Presence. I have known thee often when, as thy Friend and Physician, I have taken thee to My bosom, and healed thy sores. Alas, thou hast in the end forsaken Me! I know thee now only as a judge knows the criminal. With the eyes of My indignation I recognise thee only to be compelled to say, Henceforth, and for ever, I know thee not."

May we all be spared the doom of hearing those tremendous words! May the Divine Mercy keep the door of grace open to us until we have "entered in" with the Bridegroom Himself! And may our Guardian Angel say of each of us when we are at the point of death,

"By the grace of God, he is *ready* for the Bridegroom; and the only door that can be closed upon him shall be that golden gate which shuts out for ever all temptation, all sin, all assaults of evil spirits, and the possibility of incurring the sentence of the Second Death." "Blessed are those servants whom the Lord, when He cometh, shall find watching" (Luke xii. 37).

THE END.

LONDON:
ROBSON AND SONS, PRINTERS, PANCRAS ROAD, N.W.

BURNS, OATES, & CO.'S LIST.

THE THREE MISSION BOOKS,

Comprising all that is required for general use; the cheapest books ever issued.

1. *Complete Book of Devotions and Hymns: Path to Heaven*, 1000 pages, 2s. This Volume forms the Cheapest and most Complete Book of Devotions for Public or Private use ever issued. (25th Thousand.) Cloth, Two Shillings. Also in various bindings.
2. *Complete Choir Manual (Latin) for the Year*, 230 pieces. 10s. 6d.
3. *Complete Popular Hymn and Tune Book (English)*, 250 pieces. 10s. 6d. Melodies alone, 1s. Words, 3d.; cloth, 5d.

Prayers of St. Gertrude and Mechtilde. Neat cloth, lettered, 1s. 6d.; Fr. morocco, red edges, 2s.; best calf, red edges, 4s.; best morocco, plain, 4s. 6d.; gilt, 5s. 6d. Also in various extra bindings. On thin *vellum paper* at the same prices.

Devotions for the "Quarant' Ore," or New Visits to the Blessed Sacrament. Edited by Cardinal Wiseman. 1s., or in cloth, gilt edges, 2s.; morocco, 5s.

Imitation of the Sacred Heart. By the Rev. Father ARNOLD, S.J. 12mo, 4s. 6d.; or in handsome cloth, red edges, 5s.; also in calf, 8s; morocco, 9s.

Manual of the Sacred Heart. New edition, 2s.; red edges, 2s. 6d.; calf, 5s.; morocco, 5s. 6d.

The Spirit of St. Theresa. 2s.; red edges, with picture, 2s. 6d.

The Spirit of the Curé d'Ars. 2s. Ditto, ditto. 2s. 6d.

The Spirit of St. Gertrude. 2s. 6d.

Manna of the New Covenant; Devotions for Communion. Cloth, 2s.; bound, with red edges, 2s. 6d.

A'Kempis. The Following of Christ, in four books; a new translation, beautifully printed in royal 16mo, with borders round each page, and illustrative engravings after designs by German artists. Cloth, 3s. 6d.; calf, 6s. 6d.; morocco, 8s.; gilt, 10s. 6d. The same, pocket edition. Cloth, 1s.; bound, roan, 1s. 6d.; calf, 4s.; morocco, 4s. 6d.

Spiritual Combat; a new translation. 18mo, cloth, 3s.; calf, 6s.; morocco, 7s. The same, pocket size. Cloth, 1s.; calf, neat, 4s.; morocco, 4s. 6d.

---o---

BURNS, OATES, & CO., 63 PATERNOSTER ROW, E.C.

Missal. New and Complete Pocket Missal, in Latin and English, with all the new Offices and the Proper of Ireland, Scotland, and the Jesuits. Roan, embossed gilt edges, 4s. 6d.; calf flexible, red edges, 7s. 6d.; morocco, gilt edges, 8s. 6d.; ditto, gilt, 10s.

Epistles and Gospels for the whole Year. 1s. 6d.

Vesper Book for the Laity. This Volume contains the Office of Vespers (including Compline and Benediction), complete for *every day in the year.* Roan, 3s. 6d.; calf, 5s. 6d.; morocco, 6s. 6d.

The Psalter in Latin, 1s. 6d. *Do. in English.* New edition (*in the press*).

Easter in Heaven. By Father WENINGER, S.J. 4s. 6d.

The Spirit of Christianity. From the French of NEPVEU. 4s.

Considerations on the World. By PIOT. 1s. 6d.

The Touchstone of Character. By the Abbé CHASSAY. 3s.

Crasset. Meditations for every Day in the Year. From the French of Père CRASSET, S.J. 8vo, 8s.

Sancta Sophia. By Father BAKER, O.S.B. 5s.

Lombez on Christian Joy. 1s. 9d.

Spirit of St. Francis of Sales. 8s. 6d.

Our Faith the Victory. By Dr. McGILL. 10s.

Spiritual Maxims of St. Vincent de Paul. 1s. 4d.

The Beauties of the Sanctuary. From the French of LEBON. 2s. 6d.

The Art of Suffering. From the French of St. GERMAIN. 1s. 6d.

Method of Meditation. By Father ROOTHAN. 2s.

The Genius of Christianity. By CHATEAUBRIAND. Complete edition. 8s.

The Martyrs. By the same. 6s.

Hecker (Rev. J. T.). Aspirations of Nature. 5s.—Questions of the Soul. 4s. 6d.

Mission and Duties of Young Women. 2s. 6d.

Guide for Catholic Young Women. By Father DESHON. 4s.

Maynard on the Teaching of the Jesuits. 3s.

Mary, Star of the Sea. 3s. 6d.

Paradise of the Christian Soul. Complete. 6s.

The Words of Jesus. Edited by the Rev. F. CASWALL. 1s.

Lyra Liturgica: Verses for the Ecclesiastical Seasons. By Canon OAKELEY. 3s. 6d.

———o———

BURNS, OATES, & CO., 17 & 18 PORTMAN STREET, W.

Select Sacred Poetry. 1s.
Instructions in Christian Doctrine. 3s.
Letters on First Communion. 1s.
Flowers of St. Francis of Assisi. 3s.
Manual of Practical Piety. By St. FRANCIS DE SALES. 3s. 6d.
Manresa; or the Spiritual Exercises of St. Ignatius. 3s.
The Christian Virtues. By St. ALPHONSUS. 4s.
Eternal Truths. By the same. 3s. 6d.
On the Passion. By the same. 3s.
Jesus hath loved us. By the same. 9d.
Reflections on Spiritual Subjects. By the same. 2s. 6d.
Glories of Mary. By the same. New edition.
The Raccolta of Indulgenced Prayers. 3s.
Rodriguez on Christian Perfection. Two vols. 6s.
Stolberg's Little Book of the Love of God. 2s.
The Treasure of Superiors. 3s. 6d.
Archbishop Hughes' Complete Works. Two vols. 8vo, 24s.
Sermons. By Father BAKER. With Memoir. 8vo, 10s.
Devout Instructions on the Sundays and Holidays. By GOFFINE. 8vo, 9s. 6d.
Sermons by the Paulists of New York. First Series, 4s.; 2d ditto, 6s.; 3d ditto, 5s. 6d.; 4th ditto, 6s.; 5th ditto (1865-6), 7s.
A Hundred Short Sermons. 8vo, 8s.
Preston's Sermons. 7s.
Spalding's (Bishop) *Evidences.* 7s.
Spalding's (Bishop) *Miscellanies.* 12s. 6d.
The Gentle Sceptic. By Father WALLWORTH. A Treatise on the Authority and Truth of the Scriptures, and on the Questions of the Day as to Science, &c. 6s.
Family Devotions for every Day in the Week, with occasional Prayers. Selected from Catholic Manuals, ancient and modern. Foolscap, limp cloth, red edges, very neat, 2s.
Aids to Choirmasters in the Performance of Solemn Mass, Vespers, Compline, and the various Popular Services in General Use.

P.S. Messrs. B. & Co. will be happy to send any of the above Books on inspection.

A large allowance to the Clergy.

———o———

BURNS, OATES, & CO., 63 PATERNOSTER ROW, E.C.

RELIGIOUS BIOGRAPHY AND HISTORY.

St. Aloysius Gonzaga. 5s.
St. Charles Borromeo. 3s. 6d.
St. Vincent de Paul. 3s.
St. Francis de Sales. 3s.
The Curé d'Ars. 4s.
St. Thomas of Canterbury.
Wykeham, Waynflete, & More. 4s.
The Blessed Henry Suso. 4s.
M. Olier of Saint Sulpice. 4s.
The Early Martyrs. 3s. 6d.
St. Dominic and the Dominican Order. 8s. 6d.
Madame Swetchine. 7s. 6d.
The Sainted Queens. 3s.
Blessed John Berchmans. 2s.
St. Francis Xavier. 2s.
St. Philip Neri. 3s.
St. Ignatius. 2s.
St. Francis of Rome. 2s.
Heroines of Charity. 2s. 6d.
Saints of the Working Classes. 1s. 4d.
Sœur Rosalie and Mdlle. Lamourous. 1s.
St. Francis and St. Clare. 1s.
Lives of Pious Youth. 3s. 6d.
Modern Missions in the East and West. 3s.
Missions in Japan and Paraguay. 3s.
Religious Orders, Sketches of. 4s. 6d.
The Knights of St. John. 3s. 6d.
Anecdotes and Incidents. 2s.
Remarkable Conversions. 2s. 6d.
Pictures of Christian Heroism. 3s.
Popular Church History. 3s.
Missions in India. 5s.
Lives of the Roman Pontiffs. By DE MONTOR. Fine engravings. 2 very large vols. 58s. (cash, 50s.).
Darras' History of the Church. 4 vols. Edited by Bp. Spalding. Imperial 8vo. 2l. 8s. (cash, 2l.).
Butler's Lives of the Saints. 4 vols. cloth, 30s.
The Life of Bishop Borie. 2s.

The Life of Mary Ann of Jesus, the Lily of Quito. 3s. 6d.
Life of St. Ignatius. By BARTOLI. 2 vols. 14s.
St. Ignatius and his Companions. 4s.
The Life of Abulchar Bisciarah. 2 vols. 3s. 6d.
Life of Mme. de Soyecourt. 3s.
Life of St. Angela Merici. 3s. 6d.
Life of St. Margaret of Cortona. 3s. 6d.
Life of Princess Borghese. 2s.
Life of F. Maria Ephraim. 5s.
Life of Mrs. Seton. 8s. 6d.
Life of Mme. de la Peltrie. 2s.
Life of Father Felix de Andreis. 4s. 6d.
Life of St. Stanislaus. 1s. 6d.
Life of St. Philomena. 2s. 6d.
Life of St. Cecilia. By GUERANGER. 6s.
Lives of Fathers of the Desert. 4s. 6d.
Life of Bishop Bruté. 3s. 6d.
Life of Pius VI. 3s.
Life of St. Bridget. 2s. 6d.
Life of St. Mary Magdalen. 2s. 6d.
Life of St. Zita. 3s.
Life of St. Francis of Assisi. 2s.
Life of St. Catherine of Sienna. 6s.
Life of Bishop Flaget. 4s. 6d.
Life of Dr. Maginn. 4s. 6d.
Life of Cath. M'Auley, Foundress of the Sisters of Mercy. 10s. 6d.
Shea (J. G.). Perils of the Ocean and Wilderness. 3s. 6d.
Shea (J. G.). Missions in the United States. 9s.
Shea (J. G.). History of the Church in America. 7s. 6d.
Indian Sketches. By DE SMET. 2s. 6d.
History of the Society of Jesus. By DAURIGNAC. 2 vols. 12s. 6d.

BURNS, OATES, & CO., 17 & 18 PORTMAN STREET, W.

www.ingramcontent.com/pod-product-compliance
Lightning Source LLC
Chambersburg PA
CBHW030745230426
43667CB00007B/850